CHINA:
SEARCH FOR
COMMUNITY

CHINA:
SEARCH FOR COMMUNITY

Raymond L. and Rhea M. Whitehead

Friendship Press
New York

ACKNOWLEDGMENTS

For permission to quote copyrighted material, grateful acknowledgment is made to:

Chapter II
   Routledge, Kegan and Paul for selection from J. Macgowan, *Sidelights on China Life.*
   McClelland and Stewart for selection from Prince Kung in Jason Wong, ed., *China in the Nineteenth Century.*
   Sloan for selection from White and Jacoby, *Thunder Out of China.*
   The Atlantic Monthly for selection from Harriet C. Mills, "Thought Reform."

Chapter III
   Christian Century for selection from Alan Geyer, "Reverence for Life in China and America."
   Monthly Review Press for selection from Goldwasser and Dowty, *Huan-Ying: Workers' China.*

Chapter V
   Christian Century for selections from Eugene L. Stockwell, "The Life of Christianity in China."

Jonathan Chao for selection from "The Spirit of God at Work in China" (China Graduate School of Theology, Inc.).

Paulist Press for selection by Domenico Grasso, S.J., in Michael Chu, ed., *The New China: A Catholic Response.*

The United Church Observer for selections by E. H. Johnson and Earl Wilmott.

The Witness Magazine for selection by Carman St. J. Hunter.

CMS Newsletter for selection by Simon Barrington Ward.

One World for selection by Jonas Jonson.

CONTENTS

CHRONOLOGY

B.C.	**551 - 479**	Life of Confucius
	214	Great Wall completed
A.D.	**635**	Nestorian Christian mission begins two centuries of work in China
	1279 - 1292	Marco Polo in China
	1582	Matteo Ricci, Roman Catholic missionary, arrives in China
	1644 - 1911	Ch'ing (Manchu) Dynasty
	1683	Taiwan absorbed into Chinese empire
	1784	First American ship calls at Chinese port. Sino-American trade begins
	1807	Robert Morrison, first Protestant missionary, arrives at Canton
	1811	First American Missionary arrives in China
	1839 - 1842	Britain defeats China in Opium War. First of unequal treaties
	1850 - 1864	Taiping Rebellion

1864	10,000 Chinese indentured laborers are recruited to work on US transcontinental railroad
1881	Chinese indentured laborers begin work on Canadian Pacific Railway
1895	Japan defeats China in Sino-Japanese War. Japan obtains Taiwan and other concessions
1899 - 1900	Boxer Rebellion
1911 - 1912	Overthrow of Ch'ing (Manchu) Dynasty and establishment of new republic under Sun Yat-sen
1919	Versailles Peace Treaty leads to May Fourth Movement in China
1921	Communist Party founded in Shanghai
1934 - 1935	Long March
1937	Japan invades China
1945	Japan surrenders
1946 - 1949	Civil War between Nationalists and Communists
1949	Victorious Communists establish People's Republic of China. Nationalist government under Chiang Kai-shek retreats to Taiwan Province
1950	Korean War breaks out. US Seventh Fleet moves into Taiwan Straits
1952	Land reform completed in China
1958	Rural communes organized. Great Leap Forward
1965	Canadians go to China as language teachers
1966 - 1969	Cultural Revolution
1970	Canada establishes diplomatic relations with China
1971	United Nations votes to seat People's Republic of China
1972	Nixon trip to China. Shanghai Communique issued
1976	Deaths of Chou En-lai and Mao Tse-tung. Appointment of Hua Kuo-feng as Mao's successor. Overthrow of "Gang of Four," which included Mao's widow

FOREWORD

Robert McAfee Brown
Professor of Ecumenics and World Christianity
Union Theological Seminary

On my first visit to Hong Kong in February 1975, Ray Whitehead drove me high up into the hills behind the city and pointed westward. The hills in the far, far distance, he told me, were in the People's Republic of China.

Those hills were elusive, mysterious, far away, and (for me at least, at that moment) unreachable. I wanted very much to know what was going on beyond them, as I have for many years, particularly since the victory achieved in 1949 by the people united behind Mao.

Doors are opening, and groups of people are now visiting China. They come back and almost always their reports are enthusiastic. They have seen things that force them to revise their earlier opinions about: (a) communism, (b) democracy, (c) the role of the church, (d) all of the above and almost everything else. Most of us have not had the privilege of such a trip. And yet we need some kind of equivalent. How are we to gain an informed point of view about what is happening in China today?

The present book by Ray and Rhea Whitehead comes about as close as we are likely to get, short of a visit ourselves. Particularly valuable about their text is that it combines expertise (both of them are professional China experts, know the language, have visited the country) with an ability to communicate. They have also interspersed their own reflections with reports and critiques by others. They manage to combine what might be called critical distance with human engagement. Distance alone could be antiseptic and "safe." Engagement alone could be biased and unreliable. But the two together make a potent and exciting combination.

The book has a clear organizing principle—it describes China in terms of the "search for community." It puts that search in the history and experience of the Chinese people, and then describes the extraordinary level of human service that motivates the Chinese people today, in ways that make it hard for us to find counterparts in our Western and supposedly "Christian" culture. China, we are told, "is an oil-exporting country without any oil millionaires." A rarity, the Whiteheads call it. It is not only a rarity, it is unheard of elsewhere. How can there be a modern culture that does not let a few make most of the profit? Isn't that one of the rules of the game? The Chinese say "no."

The example suggests an area the Whiteheads explore in detail: how do we relate the rights of society as a whole to the rights of individuals within that society? China, they report, with ample documentation and evidence, gets high marks on the first alternative. It really does provide such basics as food, shelter, clothing, education and medical care for all, regardless of age, sex, class, influence or ability to pay. It does not do as well on the second. But it forces us to ask how well we have done on the first; in our laudable attention to the individual rights of protest, dissent, free speech and so forth, have we not tended to look on medical care, clothing, shelter, education and food as privileges rather than rights, lavishly available to those who can pay for them, and only grudgingly given to others, often under protest that such concessions sound a little "socialistic"?

The latter part of the book offers a fascinating description and assessment of the place of religion in general, and Christianity in particular, in China today, followed by a spectrum of four ways of viewing China theologically: affirming the need for a "visible Church" in China; seeing God's work in history being mediated through non-Christians as well as Christians; emphasizing the Christian dimension of the "values" that are emerging in China; and using China as a "mirror" through which to see ourselves more clearly.

I am writing this foreword in New York City—a long way from China. And yet, after having read this book, I feel considerably "closer" to China than I did on that Hong Kong hilltop not too long ago. The book has been of great help to me. It can be to other readers as well. Turn the page and begin . . . .

PREFACE

Why should Christians study China—land of Mao, revolution, socialism, communes, Red Guards, and acupuncture? Don't we know enough about it already? Since there are no missionaries in China, how does it relate to mission study? Towards what action does such a study lead?

Changes in China—"barefoot doctors," bosses working in the factories, workers involved in management, a poor country providing food and development for its people, Cultural Revolution, ballets about guerrilla fighters—arouse a general interest in the country. All these "strange" phenomena can become understandable and human for us.

Understanding China can lead to reflection on its significance to us as Christians. The very fact that the People's Republic of China is doing so many interesting things but no longer has missionaries or any very prominent church life challenges us to think in new ways about mission and the church's life. We can become open-minded enough to learn from those outside our faith.

It has been pointed out that the Chinese people comprise about one-fourth of the world's population. Christians of all kinds in all places also make up about a fourth. There is very little overlap—only a small number of Chinese are Christians. The interaction of Chinese and Christians is something which involves half the world's people. How can we not study and reflect more?

The title of this book is *China: Search for Community.* We are looking at both how the Chinese have sought new ways of building community and the implications of these ways for our Christian life together. The first chapter, "In Search of My Neighbor," discusses similarities and differences between North America and China in our common search for community. The second chapter deals with China's attempt to renew its community life, giving an historical perspective to the struggle. Chapter Three discusses the relationship between community and individual needs and development. Chapter Four looks at human values in China as they relate to community life. In the fifth chapter we bring together a number of responses to the Chinese experience by Christians of varying backgrounds.

Obviously it is not possible to cover all viewpoints. Purposely left out are two extremes—those who idolize China and feel that Mao and his followers can do no wrong, and those ideological anti-communists who see in China only dark and demonic forces at work. By general consensus these views lack credibility. Even within the middle range there is wide variation. Christians vary not only in their assessment of China's experience but also in the theological perspectives from which they view it.

We are particularly fortunate in having a unique contribution to this book by George and Jennie Ling. Their material is included in the first and third chapters. George studied at Oberlin, Berkeley, and Yale Divinity School and received his Ph.D. from Oxford. He is an ordained minister of the United Church of Christ. Jennie studied at Berkeley and Yale Divinity School. In 1967 they decided to go back to China and for nine years lived and worked in Chengtu, Szechuan, first in a factory and later as English teachers in a teachers' college. They and their children experienced firsthand many aspects of Chinese life from the Cultural Revolution up to 1976. In that year they left China and moved to Hong Kong, Jennie's birthplace.

Another contributor is Katharine Hockin, born of Canadian missionary parents in Szechuan and herself a missionary there for some time. In later years she became director of the Ecumenical Forum of Canada, mission study and training institute in Toronto. She wrote a section of Chapter Five. The fourth chapter was prepared by Donald E. MacInnis, former China missionary, currently director of the Midwest China Study Resource Center in St. Paul, Minnesota. He has long studied contemporary China.

Eugene Stockwell, Executive Secretary of the Division of Overseas Ministries of the National Council of Churches, prepared some material for Chapter Five, and part of his report of an interview with K. H. Ting in Nanking is also reprinted. Mark Sheldon, from the United Methodist Office for the United Nations, contributed some of the ideas for Chapter One. Also included are materials compiled from a number of Christian writers on China.

In giving this variety of views it has not been our intention to confuse but to give you, the reader, the opportunity to clarify your own response to the China experience. Our hope is that this brief account gives you sufficient information to reflect on the meaning of China for a Christian understanding of community and mission.

KUNLUN

October 1935

Far above the earth, into the blue,
You, wild Kunlun, have seen
All that was fairest in the world of men.
Your three million white jade dragons in flight
Freeze the sky with piercing cold.
In summer days your melting torrents
Flood the streams and rivers,
Turning men into fish and turtles.
Who has passed judgement on the good and ill
You have wrought these thousand autumns?

To Kunlun now I say,
Neither all your height
Nor all your snow is needed.
Could I but draw my sword o'ertopping heaven,
I'd cleave you in three:
One piece for Europe,
One for America,
One to keep in the East.
Peace would then reign over the world,
The same warmth and cold throughout the globe.

Mao Tse-tung

MAO'S NOTE:

An ancient poet said: "While the three million white jade dragons were fighting, the air was filled with their tattered scales flying." Thus he described the flying snow. I have borrowed the image to describe the snow-covered mountains. In summer, when one climbs to the top of Minshan, one looks out on a host of mountains, all white, undulating as in a dance. Among the local people a legend was current to the effect that all these mountains were afire until the Monkey King borrowed a palm leaf fan and quenched the flames, so that the mountains turned white.

I

IN SEARCH OF MY NEIGHBOR

Like the lawyer in Luke's gospel, we seek to justify our lack of neighborliness and community spirit by asking the rhetorical question, "Who is my neighbor?" We know who our neighbor is, but we remain locked in our lonely shells. Newspapers and magazines tell us again and again about the crisis in community we face. Relationships have broken down across the lines of race, age, sex, and class.

Christians begin to wonder how our message seems to get so individualized and so far away from the intensely consuming issues of our life together in community. We find people seeking a sense of belonging in spiritual movements, in new religious communities, in voluntary communes, or in looking back with nostalgia to the spirit of working together against hardship which prevailed in pioneering days. Native peoples and ethnic immigrants in North America often sense a contrast between their scattered lives today and a remembered time of social cohesiveness. Regardless of memories or new experiments, life in the larger community continues to disintegrate.

Christians have a vision of community based on the Covenant of Israel and on the New Covenant of Jesus Christ. Our problem has been to relate this vision of a common life of service and justice to the modern era in which we live. As we search for the roots of our own covenant community, and as we struggle with the questions of justice and peace in

society as a whole, China's experience is relevant. Our study of China is
based not on idle curiosity but on a deep concern for our life together.
It is not that China is able to provide solutions for our problems—finding
them is our own task. China's efforts to create a new community from a
situation of chaos and exploitation, however, may give us some hints
about alternative approaches.

Consider the following story which George Ling tells of his return to
China after 20 years away and his reunion with his brother:

"My first memorable impression of the deeply human aspect of China
was the reunion with my brother, whom I hadn't seen for 20 years. The
last time I saw him, he was a vain and cocky fighter pilot of Kuomintang
(KMT) Air Force, which he joined in the early forties during the war
against Japan. His plane was shot down by the People's Liberation Army
(PLA) during the War of Liberation and he was taken a prisoner. Evidently
he did well in prison and later joined the PLA, becoming a physical education coach in the army.

"When I saw him in 1967, he was very unlike the past. His loss of vanity
and cockiness was not surprising. What was surprising was his humble but
confident attitude about his place in the society, his deep concern for
people and his dedication to his work. He did a great deal in helping us
with menial tasks—washing (which was done by hand), emptying night
soil because there was no flush toilet, cleaning our rooms, shopping and
cooking.

"We spent long hours talking. It was soon evident that he was counsel-
ling me, showing deep understanding of my hopes, fears and aspirations.
I marvelled at the transformation of my brother and thought to myself:
What happened in the prison of the PLA was not the kind of 'brain-
washing' I had read about in the papers but more like a religious conversion and a training in its ministry. For aside from the 'new being' in him,
he was deeply committed to reach out and help others."

George Ling's experience is just one example of the dedication to community life which impresses people who encounter the new China for the
first time. Obviously this comment is not the whole story of China, but
it is a dimension which excites the imagination, especially as we seek to
find the roots of our common life.

The creation and maintenance of community depends on the dedication of people to something beyond their own selfish interests. Dedication
is inspired by stories and legends, heroines and heroes, and the myths

around which a society and its values are organized. It is profitable to compare our myths and our heroes with those of the Chinese.

North Americans have the myths of the frontier, the pioneering spirit, the conquest of new worlds, and the heroic lives of cowboys and Mounties. Some North Americans look to the brave stand of Indian leaders against the never-ending onslaught of immigrants seeking land.

For Christians, memories of circuit riders, camp meetings, revivals, and frontier missionaries are central to the story. More important perhaps is the recollection of the sense of community the church engendered, enabling people to confront hardship and disaster with support from each other and a vision of a new world in the making.

The heroes of North America today are often pop singers, sports stars, and TV personalities. In the past and for some people today the hero figures are missionaries—those who go to distant and dangerous places out of love of God and people. Albert Schweitzer, Mother Teresa, and Canada's Cardinal Leger have many admirers. Other Christian heroes are those known and appreciated for commitment to political and social causes—Dietrich Bonhoeffer, Martin Luther King, Daniel and Philip Berrigan, Dom Helder Camara.

One thing these Christian hero figures have in common is that in the eyes of their followers they are dedicated and committed to a cause beyond self. In this way they contribute to the building of local or world community.

THE MASSES ARE THE REAL HEROINES AND HEROES

Chinese effort to create a new community uses hero-models. For the most part these models tend to be "ordinary" workers or farmers who have done "heroic" things. Jennie and George Ling tell of one such person they met, a woman called "Mama Lun":

"Mama Lun was virtually one of the slaves of the landlord in the old society. She and her family worked day and night all year long but got less than 40 percent of what they reaped from the land, the landlord having taken the lion's share. That was during a normal year. In times of drought, they had to borrow rice from the landlord in order to survive. The next year, aside from paying the rent in kind, they had to pay back what they had borrowed plus interest, also in kind. Virtually nothing was left for themselves. So they had to borrow again for that year. The vicious circle continued until Mama Lun either had to sell her teen-age child or be thrown into a cage filled knee-high with water with iron spikes all round so she could neither sit nor lean. She saved her teen-ager by choosing the cage but still her baby starved to death. Mama Lun was one of the very few who survived the 'water dungeon'.

"People like Mama Lun are now given dignified positions in the society and are given the task of travelling around to share their story with young people. Often teachers and students travel to Mama Lun's commune to meet her and see the water dungeon.

"When we heard her speak we sensed her unquestioned commitment to Maoism, her deep love for the Party and people, and profound dedication toward the work she was doing."

It is not difficult to understand the commitment of people like Mama Lun, nor to appreciate the impact of their stories on others. In the search for community today in China, the stories of regeneration of those mistreated in the past have an important educational function. From our distance we begin to see the meaning of Mao's statement that the masses are the real heroes. George Ling describes a fellow worker called Lao Chen ("old" Chen), whom he came to know in a factory in Chengtu:

"Lao Chen had been a rickshaw puller. He worked 14-16 hours a day and still could not make ends meet. He would have one meal and not know where the next meal was coming from. In those days, the only time the family could have a bit of meat was on the Eve of Spring Festival, the Chinese New Year. Lao Chen's father died at an early age of illness and two younger members of the family died of hunger.

"Today Chen is a master worker with a job guaranteed until he retires. Then he will get 70 percent of his pay every month until the end of his days. He has enough to feed his family and extra for decent clothes and other daily necessities. He has a bicycle and wears a gold watch and the family has special 'Sunday dinner' every week instead of once a year. Medical care is free for him and of minimal cost for his dependents. He pays only incidental fees for his children's education. In the life of Lao Chen and people like him social status, economic conditions, and political rights have been dramatically transformed."

The Maoist analysis of society makes sense to people like Mama Lun and Lao Chen, who have experienced the transition from chaos to order and from wretchedness to adequate living standards. The problem of commitment arises for the new generation. George Ling says:

"The picture in China is not always one of dedication. Some, especially among the young, who never knew what it was like in the old society, seem to have forgotten how far the Chinese people have come. It is not easy for the young to appreciate the great transformation that has taken place in China and in the lives of the Chinese people. In other words, there is a lack of concrete vindication of what they are committed to. They are looking for this vindication now.

"That is why Premier Chou En-lai's call for modernization by the end of this century stirred up tremendous enthusiasm among the Chinese people. It was not only a hope but a proposed indication of the continuing validity of that to which China is committed."

Some North Americans may be unenthusiastic about the goal of modernization in China, especially those who see our problems of community breakdown as a result of too much technology and the consumerism which seem inevitably associated with modernization. China sees the breakdown in the West not as a result of technology but as a result of extreme individualism and the insatiable greed for profit. The Chinese hope to modernize but still maintain the sense of cohesive community which they have experienced.

The problem China faces of showing a new generation the continued validity of the system of thought adopted is not that different from the problems Christians face. The Lings comment:

"The pertinent question to ask is not what the Christian is committed to. It is quite easy to draw up a list of Christian requirements. Likewise, it would be easy to draw up a list of what Marxists ought to be committed to. The question to ask, which is much more difficult to answer, is why we do not do what we ought to do, why we do not act according to our commitments.

"The relation between faith and works is complex. Faith is the source of action, providing the strength to act. The content of faith, on the other hand, is continually being put to the test in terms of the faithful person's participation and action in society. Faith is validated by personal and social impact resulting from action.

"How deep is our Christian belief? If no living transformation is witnessed, the Christian faith will be no more than an historical relic. For this reason we should pay particular attention to what the Chinese are doing in Africa, shoulder to shoulder with their African brothers and sisters, in providing medical care, building railroads, and assisting in industrial and agricultural reconstruction. Dr. Kaunda, president of Zambia, and a Christian, praises the work of the Chinese. Ironically, he says, what the Chinese are doing in Africa today is what the Christians had always tried to do but failed."

These comments bring us back, interestingly, to the situation of "missionary heroes"—this time Maoist Chinese in Africa. President Nyerere of Tanzania has also compared the Chinese with Christian missionaries and Western experts, saying that the Western Christians are often too much concerned about housing and comfort, whereas the Chinese live in simple African style. The better housing of the Westerners becomes the desire of the Africans, said Nyerere, and acquisitiveness replaces dedication to the people.

As has been pointed out, not all Chinese are heroes of simplicity in lifestyle and commitment to common goals. If they were, there would be no need for education campaigns calling for emulation of the hero-models. What can be said is that China has set out certain egalitarian goals which are important for building community. It has reduced the big gap between rich and poor which leads to social breakdown, envy, and a selfish scramble for goods. China has made dramatic progress in developing a society based on communal values. This is why the ordinary railroad workers who go to Africa are of such interest. Their lifestyle shows that these values have been inculcated to a large extent, even though many problems remain.

THREE SERMONS OF MAO TSE-TUNG

By looking at Chinese hero figures we have tried to discern the values which lie behind the Chinese search for community and how commitment to those values is exemplified. The three "most popular" articles of Mao Tse-tung, which read like sermons, spell out the values we have been discussing. They are, "Serve the People," "The Foolish Old Man Who Removed the Mountain," and "In Memory of Norman Bethune."

SERVE THE PEOPLE. Chang Szu-teh, a member of the People's Liberation Army, died in an accident while making charcoal at the revolutionary base area in Shensi in 1944. Like all the Liberation Army men, he had been working when not involved in battle. Mao's speech at a memorial meeting for Chang included the following words:

> All men must die, but death can vary in its significance. The ancient Chinese writer Szuma Chien said, "Though death befalls all men alike,

it may be weightier than Mount Tai or lighter than a feather." To die for the people is weightier than Mount Tai, but to work for the fascists and die for the exploiters and oppressors is lighter than a feather. Comrade Chang Szu-teh died for the people, and his death is indeed weightier than Mount Tai.

We hail from all corners of the country and have joined together for a common revolutionary objective. And we need the vast majority of the people with us on the road to this objective. Today we already lead base areas with a population of 91 million, but this is not enough; to liberate the whole nation more are needed. In times of difficulty we must not lose sight of our achievements, must see the bright future and must pluck up our courage. The Chinese people are suffering; it is our duty to save them and we must exert ourselves in struggle. Wherever there is struggle there is sacrifice, and death is a common occurrence. But we have the interests of the people and the sufferings of the great majority at heart, and when we die for the people it is a worthy death. Nevertheless, we should do our best to avoid unnecessary sacrifices. Our cadres must show concern for every soldier, and all people in the revolutionary ranks must care for each other, must love and help each other.

Some people have compared these words, spoken for a common person killed serving others, with the biblical words about the suffering servant in Isaiah 52 and 53. They express similar ideas about the death of a lowly person having value beyond rational measure. One can also find similarity in Isaiah's attitude toward wealth and that of the Chinese Communists. In Isaiah 53:9 it is said of the suffering servant, "They made his grave with the wicked and with a rich man in his death, although he had done no violence . . ."(RSV). Chang would have agreed that violence and wickedness are related to wealth.

The two stories are also different. Isaiah's suffering servant is wounded and beaten and dies a death which heals and redeems others. Chang died in the midst of revolutionary struggle to change oppressive structures. The relation between spiritual solutions to suffering and revolutionary action to change the conditions of suffering merits our attention. For the Christian it is not a simple either/or.

Serving the people is a basic value in China's search for community. China's ethic of service is based on the idea that personal fulfillment and meaning are found in community effort. Heroism is communally oriented. This service ethic is often referred to in statements about model communities in China, such as the farm commune at Tachai and the "frontier" community at Taching, China's first major oil-producing area.

Tachai is the best known of China's rural communes. Located in an inhospitable region, it has been able to overcome obstacles and become a very productive unit.

Tachai has its heroines and heroes. Chen Yung-kuei, an illiterate, landless peasant at the time of liberation, became its leader. Through sweat and hard work he led the people to transform the eroding hillsides by sheer physical power, building terrace walls from native stone. A group of teen-age girls who successfully built terraces became known as the Iron Girls of Tachai. Today one of the first team of Iron Girls has become the commune's chairperson.

The commune is the basis of community life in rural areas. Smaller units, production teams, elect representatives to the commune committees. At various levels people participate in decisions about developing irrigation, determining crop plantings, and improving fertilizers and also about such things as education, health care, recreation, and other community facilities. The welfare of the people is a major consideration, and the community deals with problems of the elderly, young families with children, the handicapped, and others.

Taching, China's large oil field, is a model of industrial production and organization. This frontier community was developed on the basis of self-reliance and cooperation. Wang Chin-hsi is known through China for his willingness to make sacrifices. As a drill team captain he was a model of selflessness in opening up this new area, contributing to China's move toward industrialization.

Although Tachai and Taching have been exemplary, one finds active community cooperation throughout China. A person is not left isolated with his or her own problems. Each person lives and functions within a specific community structure.

THE FOOLISH OLD MAN WHO REMOVED THE MOUNTAIN. Along with community service, perseverance in struggle is another key value in China. There is hope in the building of a new community if the people work together. At a dark time during the war against Japan, Mao inspired courage and perseverance with a speech about moving mountains:

> There is an ancient Chinese fable called "The Foolish Old Man Who Removed the Mountain." It tells of an old man who lived in northern China long, long ago and was known as the Foolish Old Man of North Mountain. His house faced south and beyond his doorway stood the two great peaks, Taihang and Wangwu, obstructing the way.

> With great determination, he led his sons in digging up these mountains, hoe in hand. Another greybeard, known as the Wise Old Man, saw them and said derisively, "How silly of you to do this! It is quite impossible

for you few to dig up these two huge mountains." The Foolish Old Man replied, "When I die, my sons will carry on; when they die, there will be my grandsons, and then their sons and grandsons, and so on to infinity. High as they are, the mountains cannot grow any higher and with every bit we dig, they will be that much lower. Why can't we clear them away?" Having refuted the Wise Old Man's wrong view, he went on digging every day, unshaken in his conviction. God was moved by this, and he sent down two angels, who carried the mountains away on their backs.

Today, two big mountains lie like a dead weight on the Chinese people. One is imperialism, the other feudalism. The Chinese Communist Party has long made up its mind to dig them up. We must persevere and work unceasingly, and we, too, will touch God's heart. Our God is none other than the masses of the Chinese people. If they stand up and dig together with us, why can't these two mountains be cleared away?

Did you think of the Christian understanding about faith's being able to move mountains? In the Chinese fable a combination of faith and hard work moves the mountain. Is this true for Christians as well? The mountains? Mao made them out to be political and social problems facing China in that period of struggle—feudalism and imperialism. Christians might similarly see the mountains as allegories for specific difficulties. In Mao's retelling of the fable the Chinese people are the ones who have the power to intervene, to reward the faith and work of the revolutionaries by using their collective strength to move the mountains.

A commitment to struggle and frugality is also considered important. Mao talked of "plain living and hard struggle" as necessary in China even after the victory of the revolution. The fable of the foolish old man gives meaning to struggle. It encourages people facing difficulties, in bad farming areas, for example, to work together to transform the earth. The people of Tachai Commune often refer to this essay of Mao's.

IN MEMORY OF NORMAN BETHUNE. The hero of the third of these articles is Canadian surgeon Norman Bethune, who went to China with United States and Canadian support to assist in the struggle against Japan. At the time Dr. Bethune was about 50 years of age and already well-known both for advances in surgical technology and for his political involvements.

Bethune died in 1939 in China after contracting blood poisoning while operating in war conditions without the protection of rubber gloves. His birthplace, a manse in Gravenhurst, Ontario, has been restored and is open as a historical site and museum.

In memory of Bethune Mao wrote:

He arrived in Yenan in the spring of last year (1938), went to work in the Wutai Mountains, and to our great sorrow died a martyr at his post. What kind of spirit is this that makes a foreigner selflessly adopt the cause of the Chinese people's liberation as his own? It is the spirit of internationalism . . . .

Comrade Bethune's spirit, his utter devotion to others without any thought of self, was shown in his great sense of responsibility in his work and his great warmheartedness towards all comrades and the people . . . . No one who returned from the front failed to express admiration for Bethune whenever his name was mentioned, and none remained unmoved by his spirit. . . .

I am deeply grieved over his death. Now we are all commemorating him, which shows how profoundly his spirit inspires everyone. We must all learn the spirit of absolute selflessness from him. With this spirit everyone can be very useful to the people. A man's ability may be great or small, but if he has this spirit, he is already noble-minded and pure, a man of moral integrity and above vulgar interests, a man who is of value to the people.

The values suggested here are selflessness and service which go beyond racial and national boundaries. The building of community is not an introverted process but one that includes neighbors everywhere.

Bethune brings to mind again the missionary image, the one who leaves home and kindred to serve in another land. Biblically we are reminded of the words of Jesus, "Greater love hath no man than this, that he lay down his life for his friends."

COMMUNITY SPIRIT AND ECONOMIC DISPARITY

Are the political and economic factors, so central to Chinese values, relevant to our spiritual search for community? Two recent newspaper articles, one from New York, the other from Toronto, suggest some dimensions of the problem.

A *New York Times* article pointed out that seven of 10 families in the United States have a 50-50 chance of spending some years in financial distress. This 70 percent of the population, dependent on wages and salaries, was considered economically vulnerable. Studies show that "individual ability and effort" do not count in determining who falls into economic difficulty. "Individual characteristics such as ambition, planning ahead, saving money, the drive to achieve—all the tested virtues—are essentially unrelated either to economic status or economic progress." Only 30 percent of the population has moved into a range where they are economically secure. That 30 percent is gaining wealth at a rate faster than inflation is growing, while the rest are going down.

Studies also show, according to this article, that "security and progress cannot be gained by individual action." People will remain vulnerable, it is suggested, "until they learn to function collectively—to act together, to get for each other, a bigger piece of the pie." Comparing this with China's experience one wonders whether community cohesiveness can be built on the basis of either a harsher struggle for a bigger piece of the pie or a decision to let the majority remain vulnerable.

A Toronto *Star* article raises the question of why people in the middle should cut back if those at the top go on getting more and more. The writer says, "I don't see any lawyers or bank presidents or politicians volunteering to lower their standard of living . . . . All I see are sleek angry politicians, all making more money than I do and then telling me I am asking for too much."

These articles give us a glimpse of the value questions we face. Economic disparities, and the scramble to get more, lead to community breakdown. The spiritual problem of building our life together in community is profoundly influenced by economic disparities. Racial, sexual, and ethnic tensions as well are all exacerbated by these economic problems.

Disparities exist in Chinese society but within a range that seems very limited when compared with North America or much of the Third World. China is an oil exporting country without any oil millionaires—a rarity. The health care system, social cohesiveness, the educational system, the neighborhood and commune life together could not exist as they do if a competitive profit motive were a central value. We may much prefer our system with its wealthy executives, orthodontists, real estate investors, pop stars and athletes. If so, we have to consider, as Christians, how our possession of or dream of wealth conflicts with our desire for a world community based on justice and peace.

II

A REVOLUTION IS NOT A PICNIC

A revolution is not a dinner party, or writing an essay, or painting a picture, or doing embroidery; it cannot be so refined, so leisurely and gentle, so temperate, kind, courteous, restrained and magnanimous. A revolution is an insurrection, an act of violence by which one class overthrows another.

—Mao Tse-tung

If Mao had been a North American he might have said a revolution is no picnic; it is not fun and games. The struggle involves a great amount of anguish, suffering, and pain. The very violence of the revolution causes some Christians to question the validity of China's development, although others point out that China's revolution was not more violent than wars and revolutions in the "Christian" West.

This chapter discusses the background of revolutionary change in China. The struggle did not begin with the Communist revolution. It was preceded by the violence of gunboats from Britain and the United States and other Western imperial powers and by the militant rise of Japan.

Two main threads run through the history of modern China's struggle. The first was the issue of *national integrity*—both geographic unity of the country and genuine independence from outside interference. The second was the problem of *human values* in a period of cultural and social disorder.

A CENTURY OF STRUGGLE

For over a hundred years prior to the establishment of the People's Republic of China in 1949 the country experienced defeat after defeat at the hands of foreign powers. China was carved up by expanding imperial nations. In the resulting chaos and oppression social values deteriorated. The central government in China fell into corruption and incompetence. People responded with a series of revolutionary and reform movements, none of which proved successful.

The decline of China in the 1800's was more severely felt, perhaps, because for thousands of years of Chinese history the Celestial Empire, the Middle Kingdom (as they called themselves) had never confronted a technologically superior enemy. To understand Chinese feelings try to imagine France invaded by Sri Lankans armed with new types of weapons and the Sri Lankans gaining control of cultural, economic, and educational life in France, insisting in a patronizing way that their Sri Lankan culture and religion were what France needed for national salvation. The French would not have taken very kindly to such a situation. China in a similar one was humiliated and angered.

Pieces of China were gradually eaten away. The British took Hong Kong, on the Pearl River estuary. The main island and harbor were ceded to the British Crown at the end of the Opium War (1839-41). How did the Opium War come about? The British East India Company was growing opium in India and selling it illegally in China. American merchants joined this drug trafficking, with all its serious debilitating effects on the Chinese. The Opium War resulted when the Chinese attempted to stop the trade by destroying a cargo of British opium in Canton. Since "British property" had been destroyed the Crown reacted with an expeditionary force which defeated the Chinese. The ensuing Treaty of Nanking in 1842 gave Hong Kong to the British and opened up various ports for trade (and opium smuggling). This was one in a series of "unequal treaties."

Through more wars and more unequal treaties further pieces of China were taken. Hong Kong increased its size twice. Russia took a large area (the size of France) from China's northern Pacific coast, which now forms the Soviet Maritime Provinces. Japan defeated China in war in 1895 and took Taiwan as a colony. Germany and France each had pieces of China under their control. All were taken by violent action against the Chinese, who were compelled to sign treaties which were simply rip-offs. Not many Christian voices protested the violence of the empire builders.

The discussion of territorial questions should not cause us to lose sight of the tremendous human problems China faced in this century of struggle. One cannot speak of the Opium War and forget the lives of individuals and families destroyed by addiction.

An Englishman, J. Macgowan, describes his visit, made out of curiosity, to an opium den in a Chinese town. He includes a retelling of these comments by the den's owner:

> The man on the next bench to him is one of the heaviest smokers in the town, and can take as much as would poison two or three beginners. He has smoked over thirty years, and now he seems to have lost all will of his own, and all ambition for anything, excepting the one passionate desire to get the opium when the craving creeps into his bones. At one time he was fairly well-to-do, but now he is a poor man. Everything he possessed was gradually disposed of to get him his daily amount of opium. His business of course was neglected and failed to support the family. By-and-by he had to sell his little son to get money to satisfy his craving, and when that was spent he disposed of his wife, and now the child is in one part of the town and his mother in another; and a happy release it was for them both," he added with a grim smile, "for the man is hopeless and could never have supported them . . . ."
>
> By the way," he added suddenly . . . , "is it not true that opium was brought to China by you English? How cruel of you people," he said with a passionate flash in his eyes, "to bring such wretchedness upon a nation that never did them any wrong!

The opium trade did violence to human life. Famine was another form of violence, not directly attributable to the foreign imperialists but certainly accentuated by the chaotic conditions resulting from foreign intervention. Millions died as a result of flood- or drought-induced famine in the latter half of the nineteenth century. Missionary Timothy Richard described a situation in which people pulled down their houses to sell every scrap of wood to buy grain. In winter these homeless ones dug deep pits where 30 or 40 people would stay in a desperate attempt to keep warm and alive. He reported seeing bodies along the road, eaten by birds and dogs, after people finally lost strength to bury the dead. Two youths of about 18 were seen "tottering on their feet, and leaning on sticks as if 90." Women from the stricken areas were taken off in carts to be sold as prostitutes and slaves.

When a people are oppressed by an alien group they often unconsciously take elements of the oppressor's world view for use in their struggle against them. Black slaves in the United States used biblical events in their freedom stories and songs. A similar thing happened in China.

The Taiping (Heavenly Peace) Rebellion (1850-1864) was one instance of an internal revolt in reaction to foreign encroachment which used the foreigners' ideology in its struggle. The roots of this revolt can be traced to China's defeat in the Opium War and resulting discontent among the people. The leader of the revolt, Hung Hsiu-ch'uan, took instruction from a missionary and was baptized. He had visions of himself as the younger brother of Jesus Christ, leading the Chinese people to freedom and development. The movement came close to turning Chinese history around in the middle of the nineteenth century. The Western powers joined with the Manchu throne in defeating the rebellion, but not before it had spread throughout southern China.

The Chinese continued to search for a way to deal with unprecedented "barbarian" power. The following document, prepared for the Emperor in 1860 by Prince Kung, indicates the growing perception of China's real peril:

> The Western barbarians, after the Treaty of Nanking, became increasingly demanding and insolent. Their savage attack on Peking this year was the culmination of this development, and it leaves no doubt whatever of the dangers confronting us arising from Western greed and aggressiveness. . . .
>
> . . . The English appear to be the most powerful, the Russians the most secretive and ambitious, and the French and Americans willing accomplices in the projects initiated by the others.
>
> . . . Your Majesty's servants are patriotic men who have never for a moment dared be forgetful of their duty to you and the nation, and they share to the bitter brim the indignation and humiliation that all men of flesh and blood feel at the arrogant, lawless behaviour of the barbarians. However, it will surely be the course of greater wisdom for all of us to remember that the barbarians were able to assert their will this year because we were preoccupied with the Nien and Taiping Rebellions, and that until we put our own house in order, another war against the foreigners will bring no better results. . . .
>
> . . . Your Majesty's servants feel that their analysis of the present situation is best expressed in medical terms. . . . The Russians share a long border with us, and they have been actively seeking piecemeal acquisitions along our common border in the manner of a silkworm nibbling at a mulberry leaf. They should therefore be considered a potentially crippling ailment of the vital organs. The English, on the other hand, are only interested in trade. Though they are cruel and unreasonable men who must sooner or later be taken in hand if our stance before the

world is to remain firm, they do not menace the roots of our national
existence, and therefore may be treated as an illness of the limbs. ....

Unhappily for Prince Kung's plan, China's leaders had neither the time
nor the ability to put their own house in order. The Ching Dynasty never
recovered from the Taiping Rebellion, and it faded away as much from its
own inner weakness as from the revolutionary forces aligned against it.
Several decades later in 1894-95, China suffered another defeat and had
to cede Taiwan to Japan as a colony. At the same time German exploitation in Shantung and special privileges for Catholic missionaries secured by
pressure from France combined to give cause for another uprising, the
Boxer Rebellion. In contrast with the Taipings, the Boxers were vehe-
mently anti-Christian and anti-foreign. In 1900 the Boxers in Peking killed
a number of missionaries as a wave of anti-foreignism swept the country.
At a throne conference in the midst of these events, the government
minister is reported to have said:

> In the decades since China established relations with the outside world,
> almost never has a single year passed without some incident involving
> the Christians. Such incidents have always been settled either by con-
> ciliation or compensation. What the Boxers are now pushing us into,
> however, is the killing of properly accredited diplomats in retaliation
> for wrongs committed by the Christians and their missionaries.

Again, according to established pattern, a foreign army subdued the
rebellion, rescued the foreigners, looted the city, and wrung huge indem-
nities in gold from the beleaguered Chinese.

The defeat of the Boxers increased foreign involvement in China's
affairs. Ten foreign nations now maintained themselves by force in Peking.
Revolutionary activity escalated. The next round again turned to the
culture and ideas of the oppressors. Sun Yat-sen was the leader of the new
revolutionary activity. He was a Christian, educated in Hawaii. Sun's birthplace was an old Taiping stronghold and in many ways he carried on the
violent revolution begun there. He wanted democracy, independence, and
socialist reforms.

The 1911 revolution, which ended the last dynasty, broke out while
Sun Yat-sen was in exile in England. He hurriedly returned to China to
take up leadership. He was never able to achieve national unity. Regional
rulers had already become strong under the Manchus, and these "war
lords" exercised power for the next several decades, with central leadership always tenuous.

The fall of the Ching or Manchu dynasty in 1911 did not end China's territorial problems. In 1919 China suffered defeat again, this time diplomatic, at Versailles. The Treaty of Versailles in that year gave the German-controlled areas of Shantung Province to Japan. This move was a betrayal of the Chinese, who supported the allies in World War I. The bitterness over this betrayal led to one of the most important outbreaks of student protest in Chinese history, the May Fourth movement. A whole range of cultural and educational reforms flowed from this Movement with far-reaching impact down to the present. The tasks of achieving national integrity and a more human society still remained. Mao Tse-tung, Chou En-lai, and other young radical students nurtured in the May Fourth Movement emerged as leaders of the revolutionary struggle which finally dealt with these problems.

At Sun Yat-sen's death in 1925, Chiang Kai-shek became leader of the Kuomintang (KMT) or Nationalist Party. Chiang Kai-shek was a strange mixture of traditional and modern. His thinking was in many ways feudal, but he became a baptized Christian nevertheless. Again, he seemed to use foreign ideas to fight the foreigners.

In alliance with the Communists, Chiang sought to unify the country. The alliance made it possible for Chiang to take Shanghai in 1927. The Communist workers' organization in Shanghai provided the shock force from within, bringing a quick victory for the united forces. Chiang immediately turned on his allies, however, beheading many of the Communists who had participated in the battle. The urban-based Communist movement was broken, setting the scene for a crucial turn of events—Mao's decision to build the revolutionary struggle on the basis of the peasants, as the Taipings had done.

Some Christian missionaries were aware of Chiang's plan to turn against the Communists. An American Methodist bishop in China wrote with pride that the Chiangs were staying at a mission compound prior to the march on Shanghai. Madame Chiang was taking English lessons from one of the missionary women. This intimate relationship brought out the information that a split was imminent, much to the delight of the missionaries. Many missionaries supported Chiang Kai-shek's violent revolution because he seemed willing to allow missionary work to go on undisturbed. They were afraid the left-wing revolutionaries would control mission and educational work and criticize missions for standing on the side of wealth, property, and imperialism.

When the split came, the missionaries reported on Communist atrocities but remained silent about hundreds beheaded by Chiang Kai-shek's forces.

When the Russian adviser Borodin was forced to flee, an American Methodist bishop wrote, "I would enjoy pulling the string which would release a good-sized bomb from an aeroplane over his head." Another bishop wrote, "God help Chiang Kai-shek and the Right Wing to eliminate this gang of world revolutionaries, who are largely responsible for the present chaos."

Arguments raged among the missionaries and their home churches about the extent of the "Bolshevik" influence in the Chinese revolution and the threat of Communism to the missionary enterprise in China. They were concerned about maintaining "a place for Christianity in China's future civilization."

Meanwhile, China's problems of national decline and deteriorating social values continued. Japan moved into Manchuria in 1931. In the ensuing war Japan controlled large portions of China's eastern coastal provinces.

Journalist Theodore White described famine conditions aggravated by the corruption and incompetence of Chiang Kai-shek's bureaucracy during this war period:

> There were corpses on the road. A girl of no more than seventeen, slim and pretty, lay on the damp earth, her lips blue with death; her eyes were open and the rain fell on them. People chipped bark, pounded it by the roadside for food; vendors sold leaves at a dollar a bundle. A dog, digging at a mound, was exposing a human body. Ghostlike men were skimming the stagnant pools to eat the green slime of the waters.
>
> . . . The Chinese government failed to foresee the famine; when it came, it failed to act until too late. . . . Stupidity and inefficiency marked the relief effort. But the grisly tragedy was compounded even further by the actions of the constituted local authorities. The peasants, as we saw them, were dying. They were dying on the roads, in the mountains, by the railway stations, in their mud huts, in the fields. And as they died, the government continued to wring from them the last possible ounce of tax. . . . No excuses were allowed; peasants who were eating elm bark and dried leaves had to haul their last sack of seed grain to the tax collector's office. . . .

The catalogue of the dehumanizing aspects of China's experience could go on and on. Obviously it is not the whole story of what was happening in China, but large segments of the population experienced extreme poverty which sometimes forced them to sell their children, exploitative working conditions in factories or in agriculture, child labor for long hours seven days a week, impossible indebtedness to usurers, humiliation of peasant women at the hands of those with wealth, bitter competitive struggle just to stay alive, and degrading treatment by foreigners. In the International Settlement in Shanghai, for example, an infamous sign was posted on the entrance to a park: DOGS AND CHINESE NOT ALLOWED.

MAO AND THE RISE OF CHINA

Born in 1893, Mao was a student when the 1911 revolution took place and in his twenties during the May Fourth Movement of 1919. He was a founding member of the Chinese Communist Party in 1921, and he took the lead in building a peasant-based movement after Chiang Kai-shek's purge of 1927.

For Mao, Marxist revolution became the key for solving the problems of national integrity and human values. Reflecting on China's struggle, he wrote:

> For a hundred years, the finest sons and daughters of the disaster-ridden Chinese nation fought and sacrificed their lives, one stepping into the breach where another fell, in quest of the truth that would save the country and the people. This moves us to song and tears. But it was only after World War I and the October Revolution that we found Marxism-Leninism, the best of truths, the best of weapons for the liberation of our nation.

Mao was not different from other dedicated Chinese in his desire to find a way to save the nation and the people. Marxism appealed because it opposed the forces which were clearly the source of Chinese misery— foreign imperialism on the one hand, and corrupt, inhuman economic oppression on the other.

The turbulent revolution led by Mao has become legendary. A new base was established in the Chingkang Mountains in south central China. Surrounded by Chiang's forces, Mao's army launched out on the Long March in 1934, covering six thousand miles of China's most rugged terrain in about a year's time. A new base area was established at Yenan, in the desolate Northwest. Years of hardship and struggle tempered the Maoist leaders and established the values of frugality, simplicity, and the dignity of physical labor which continue to this day.

From Yenan the Maoists fought against the invading Japanese. They established a new alliance with Chiang Kai-shek in the common effort against this intruding power. After the defeat of Japan, Nationalists and Communists attempted to find a peaceful resolution of their differences, but hostilities broke out again in a renewed civil war. Given the circumstances of these several decades, it is not surprising that Mao wrote the words, "A revolution is not a dinner party," and, "Political power grows out of the barrel of a gun." Future historians may well argue that one of the great turning points of the twentieth century was the Maoist victory in 1949. Four years before, at the end of the Pacific war, few would have dared predict such rapid and complete success for the People's Liberation Army under Mao. At the beginning of this phase, the Maoists were in an inferior position in geography, numbers, and weapons. It is not to discount the very real brilliance of Mao's military strategy to say that it was a victory which can be explained only on the basis of the will of the people. The people had lost confidence in the corrupt and cruel policies of the Nationalists under Chiang Kai-shek and saw in the People's Liberation Army the one hope for China.

On October 1, 1949, Mao ascended the rostrum at Tien-an-men, the Gate of Heavenly Peace, in Peking and proclaimed the establishment of the People's Republic of China. "The Chinese people have stood up," Mao said, and few would disagree.

The establishment of the People's Republic of China did not mean that the problems of national integrity and the renewal of values and culture had been totally solved. With the defeat of Japan in 1945 Hong Kong went back under British control. Macao continued under Portugal. Taiwan was returned to China at the end of World War II but then in the new civil war became an island retreat for Chiang Kai-shek. Before the unification of China could be completed the Korean War broke out and American military power intervened in Taiwan and Taiwan Straits. Some small islands went back to Chinese control but not Quemoy, Matsu, the Pescadores, and Taiwan itself. Taiwan is the main area where Western power still prevents the achievement of Chinese national integrity, but Macao, Hong Kong, and some Sino-Soviet border areas also remain as unsolved problems from the era of unequal treaties.

The revitalization of culture and values was not accomplished at a stroke in 1949 either. In fact, the outstanding feature of Chinese history in the past three decades, along with the struggle for production, has been the continuing attempt to transform values.

THE TRANSFORMATION OF VALUES

The struggle to revolutionize values is no picnic either. To transform values the Chinese used, among other things, a method of criticism and self-criticism. It entails many meetings in small groups to discuss values and commitment and what, in practice, one is doing about them. This method is still used today, although its role was more visible in the transition period of the early 1950's when many intellectuals from diverse backgrounds were coming to terms with the new social values introduced by Mao and his followers.

Harriet Mills, who was imprisoned by the Communists, discussed the reasons the method was so effective:

> Most important of all . . . is a sense of nationalism, a patriotic pride in China's new posture of confidence and achievement. . . . This pride, in turn, has generated a remarkably effective and spontaneous code of public honesty, courtesy, and civic sense unknown in the old China. . . . As a professor of English . . . explained to me in the spring of 1951, "Now we can again be proud to be Chinese!"

> The man, a master of arts from Yale, had taught in an army language program at Harvard during World War II and knew and liked America. No left-wing enthusiast, he was slow in making up his mind about the Communists in the early period of their power, but when they brought the country under control, licked inflation, improved material conditions in the universities, and dared abrogate the unequal treaties, he proudly identified himself with the new China. For him, group study was stimulating. He looked on it as accelerating the weeding out of his undesirable bourgeois liberalism and promoting the growth of new socialist thinking. . . .

Although a great surge of moral revitalization occurred in the years immediately after the establishment of the new government, people came to realize that backsliding, laziness, corruption, and selfishness were enduring problems. A system of campaigns for moral renewal has characterized the Chinese scene. These campaigns are not dissimilar to renewal movements which have taken place in the church throughout the centuries.

The most outstanding campaign came in the late 1960's, the Great Proletarian Cultural Revolution, as it was called. This Cultural Revolution emphasized community interest, anti-elitism, commitment to revolutionary social goals, dignity of manual labor, equality of women and men, and education for the common people.

No easy or final answers emerged from the Cultural Revolution, but many important advances were made. Educational structures were reformed to improve the proportional representation of workers and peasants among university students. Participation of officials, artists, teachers, and others in manual labor was promoted to counteract elitism. Health care delivery in the rural areas was improved. The next two chapters describe and comment on many of these changes.

Moral campaigns have continued in the 1970's, especially the anti-Confucius campaign, which again attacked elitism in the government and Party. This campaign also criticized male chauvinism. The year 1976 was a crucial one for China. The deaths that year of Mao Tse-tung, Chou En-lai and Chu Teh, all three founders of the Communist Revolution, moved China into a new era of "second generation" leadership. It is still too soon to tell how this change will affect the moral drive of the nation. Immediately after Mao's death the "Gang of Four" was purged for attempting to take power. This "gang" included Mao's wife, Chiang Ching. Criticism of the Gang of Four turned into a general moral and cultural movement.

There is no reason to assume that campaigns for moral renewal will cease. Many people have grasped Mao's vision of continuous struggle against selfishness. Such people are striving to build a new society in which all will work and all will have access to cultural and material resources. The ongoing revolution to create such a society will never be a picnic. To avoid this struggle, to ignore the moral issues, to resign oneself to "inevitable" exploitation and oppression is no picnic either, not, at least for the vast majority at the bottom.

CHANGSHA

1925

Alone I stand in the autumn cold
On the tip of Orange Island,
The Hsiang flowing northward;
I see a thousand hills crimsoned through
By their serried woods deep-dyed,
And a hundred barges vying
Over crystal blue waters.
Eagles cleave the air,
Fish glide in the limpid deep;
Under freezing skies a million creatures contend in
    freedom.
Brooding over this immensity,
I ask, on this boundless land
Who rules over man's destiny?

I was here with a throng of companions
Vivid yet those crowded months and years.
Young we were, schoolmates,
At life's full flowering;
Filled with student enthusiasm
Boldly we cast all restraints aside.
Pointing to our mountains and rivers,
Setting people afire with our words,
We counted the mighty no more than muck.
Remember still
How, venturing midstream, we struck the waters
And waves stayed the speeding boats?

Mao Tse-tung

III
COMMUNITY AND THE SEARCH FOR SELF

In the previous chapter we reflected on the historical sweep of the Chinese revolution and the continuing campaigns for moral renewal. A question often raised by North Americans is how this revolutionary development and moral renewal relates to personal freedom. How does the organization of Chinese society, the collective spirit and style of life, affect individuals? Many are uneasy. We say "hurray," "yes" for all that has been accomplished—the feeding of people, restoration of dignity, provision of education and health care. But questions of whether the individual can find self-fulfillment in "serving the people" remain. Many grant that the rights of the *community* to health care and education have been basically assured but ask about the "rights of the *individual*."

The Chinese have moved firmly and steadily to restrict privileges enjoyed by only an elite so that all may more equally share society's resources. But, one might ask, in the process of seeking greater social justice, have not the Chinese stifled the creative, free spirits of people? What about coercion and lack of privacy?

Some questions have no easy answers. This chapter, in looking at the experiences and observations of several people, tries to show how some Chinese feel and how some Westerners have grappled with such questions.

John Helliker, a Canadian exchange student in Peking for two years, lived at Peking University with a Chinese roommate. John observes:

If I were to emphasize one aspect [of the life of university students] it would be their participation in a cohesive group (through classes, sports, work, fun). There is no doubt in my mind that this participation helps them learn more effectively and *develop as individuals.* The latter comment may seem strange to some. But these students, through their daily contact and work together and their friendships, learn what it is to be responsible for themselves and other people. . . . They used to hold class discussions in the room next to mine. If I wanted to get any work done that night I would have to go somewhere else because the debates they had were so lively and loud that I couldn't resist just sitting and listening to them. . . .

Are students exceptional? George and Jennie Ling wrote the following pages about their experience while living in a Chinese factory community.

We consider the time spent in a factory in Chengtu in the southwestern part of China to be some of the most fulfilling years in our lives. Why? Perhaps because we felt so at one with the other workers there. We had no need to put up a front, no need to keep up with the Joneses, no fear of loneliness or anxiety over non-acceptance. We felt we could give ourselves completely. Start with personal belongings. We tried not to let them come between us and others. Our camera was out of the house more often than in; our bicycle was always available for others. The door of our apartment was always open. In fact, the whole floor where four families lived was like one big apartment. During meal times, members of one family might go to another to sample their food. Sometimes another family would bring their bowls and eat with us. The three-year-old girl from next door virtually became our fourth child at meal times.

When the weather was not too warm as many as 12 or 13 people might jam into one of our 10 X 12 rooms. Spirited debate and hilarity filled the room!

During the hot summer months, everyone went outdoors after supper. The open courtyards in the residential areas of our factory compound were filled with people. Some played basketball on the lighted courts. Little children played hide and seek, sang, and folk danced. Others devoured illustrated stories similar to comics.

Further away from the basketball court a few sat in bamboo easy chairs, smoking or sipping tea poured from thermoses. Soon, others joined in, bringing their own tea cups and perhaps another thermos. Talk centered around current events and real life situations. And yet the gatherings had the aura of an old storytelling session. The perceptiveness, imagination and creativity of the real-life storytellers drew large crowds. The sense of community was very live.

Chess and cards were also favorites. Gambling was not allowed, but there were many ways to "punish" losers: doing push-ups, crawling under the table, sticking paper tags on faces.

The high degree of communal living might be difficult for those used to much privacy. Actually, we found quite a bit of privacy when we needed it. We were free to do what we wanted in our free time. If we closed our doors, people respected that and left us alone.

Anxiety is often expressed that such communal life stifles creativity. We found in China that there is not much room for individual creativity in the sense that one can write books about his or her own ideas or do something completely according to an individual conception of things. There is, however, a good deal of opportunity for collective creativity. That is, whereas an individual is not encouraged to act on his or her own, there is considerable room for creativity when the person tackles a common problem in a group.

In a commune, if a group is faced with the problem of whether to increase productivity or income, everybody expresses ideas. Any work-team, as a group, can experiment with whatever they want. If a young people's group is faced with the problem of how to channel their aspirations and energies, they experiment with all sorts of ideas and activities as long as it is within the values and principles of Marxism.

In the West, self-realization for young people is usually associated with "choosing a career." The young workers in the factory in which we worked were not necessarily there out of free choice. They were assigned to the Rubber Product Manufacturing Factory after graduation from high school. But we did not think the workers' talents were stifled. For instance, when the factory found that George had an interest in technical innovation, he was given quite a free hand in thinking up projects for the factory as well as in designing and finding solutions for technical problems. He worked with young workers initially unskilled who gradually developed various skills. Some had special interest in machine design, some in mechanics. The workers who had special inclination and skills in electronics took care of the automatic control systems. Within the communally defined tasks and objectives there was room for individual expression of interest and inclinations.

In addition, there was opportunity in music and art. Sports teams played against other factories. The level of achievement in each of these groups was high. People found considerable recognition and satisfaction in them and if really talented might move from those groups into a more full-time professional status in sports or art.

When we first arrived in China we had the impression that people did not seek excitement and thrills in their recreational life as is so common in hot-rodding, skiing, hang-gliding or other North American recreational pursuits. On Sundays and holidays Chinese were content to take casual walks in the parks, take families to nearby scenic spots, or just gather with friends and relatives. After we were assigned jobs we began to realize that excitement and thrills were incorporated into the everyday working life of people. When there was a new challenge, such as creating a new product or increasing production, people got excited thinking up ways to reach the goal and tackle the problems. They were thrilled when the objective was reached.

For instance, when proposals were made to fulfill a factory's annual quota ahead of schedule, workers were excited about the prospect. Meetings were held to discuss ways to do that. An indicator showed the percentage of goods produced every day. When finally the quota was met a large red paper announcement was sent with drums and gongs to the administrative committee of the factory. Other divisions would send congratulatory notes with drums and gongs. The atmosphere was most festive.

If news came that a certain production process would be mechanized or automated, excitement filled the air. Everybody put in their two cents' worth of ideas. Success again brought a celebration.

Participating in these efforts brought home to us for the first time the difference and significance of public ownership. We had thought that, for workers, there was not much difference working under a capitalist system or a socialist one. The State was just a bigger capitalist. But later we saw that workers believed they participated in ownership in the sense that they gain from the profit of the State through medical care, educational benefits, improvements of public services, and the raising of living standards. They saw a technical innovation as bringing improvements to them rather than making more money for stockholders or creating unemployment.

So we understood more clearly why Chinese workers were able to get excitement out of daily work instead of primarily from recreational activities. In some ways it may be similar to North American frontier life when work, not recreation, provided meaning to life. Of course, there was time for recreation. On Sundays and holidays people relaxed, recuperating mentally and physically so they could tackle new problems when they went back to work.

In our experience, communal life does not mean the stifling of individual spirit but a demand for people to see themselves as parts of a whole, a demand for a sense of social responsibility. Individual aspirations are defined according to the goals of society. This did not seem to exclude individual inclination, interest or quite independent work. We read many publicized reports on contributions which came out of very intensive but quiet and individual work; we also read citations given to people who spent long lonely hours to master a skill, a language, or specialized knowledge which would make a contribution to Chinese life.

Doctors in the Chinese medical and health service are a good case in point. Doctors are not free to seek fame and fortune but to use their training and skills for service to the people. Some specialists we knew had used their skill and long years of experience to advise and help people in remote mountainous areas, in improving the knowledge and skills of local staff as well as in helping to train "barefoot doctors" (paramedics) in rural areas.

In doing this, doctors lost the freedom to select exactly what they wanted to do and where they wanted to work. But medical care in the vast rural areas of China before liberation was notoriously poor. It was even deplorable before the Cultural Revolution, when new efforts were finally made to improve it. The contributions of dedicated doctors have brought vast improvement in the access of medical care to rural people in remote parts of China.

Most Chinese find fulfilment in meeting communal needs. The communal life is, in a sense, a liberation, a freedom from preoccupation with the self, freedom from the anxieties and fears of the self struggling for existence, freedom from struggling for recognition in a competitive system.

But, we might ask, how well are human resources allocated so that people have the chance to use their training and abilities? Is each person's creativity utilized and allowed full expression? In general, we would answer yes. Yet this very much depends on the sensitivity of the cadres involved. Our job assignment was reconsidered after we made known to the Provincial Revolutionary Committee that we were not used according to the best of our ability in the factory. We were reassigned as teachers of English in a teachers' college.

Sometimes, however, cadres have not been sufficiently flexible in matching people's inclinations and talents to the tasks-at-hand. This is a

present weakness of the Chinese system. So much depends on the cadre's understanding of the Party's policy, his own dedication and organizational and administrative abilities. The emphasis on the human element is at once a strong point in the Chinese system and its weakness.

Let us come back to the question of human rights. It seems fair to say that in China the rights of society as a whole have been guaranteed, comparatively speaking, in a positive manner. Food, health care, education, work, participation in community decision-making are basically assured. Real progress has been made in upgrading the status of manual workers, women, and peasants.

On the other hand, the rights of the individual have been very much curtailed. The rights of individuals and collective rights are in tension. The Chinese position, in oversimplified terms, is to narrow the gap in the inequities in society. What they call "bourgeois rights"—privileges enjoyed by only a small number of people, an elite—are to be increasingly restricted. This policy is true for income received, access to education, any "perks" that tend to go with positions of higher responsibility. It seems to many Westerners to violate the freedom of individuals.

But let us look more closely at how China views human rights. Its approach is different from that of Western liberal democracy. Take an example from the Universal Declaration of Human Rights: "All human beings are born free and equal in dignity and human rights." Chinese would ask what this statement means. Not all are, in fact, born equal, unless it is meant equal in potential for dignity.

What are those born "less equal" to do about their lack of dignity or lack of access to the rights of food, employment, education, and health? The Declaration does not say anything about struggle, struggle against those who are born "more equal"—those whose wealth and prestige and knowledge give them greater access to power against those who are deprived of power. Paulo Freire, well-known Christian educator, has said that revolution is a basic right. The Chinese would agree. We often aren't sure.

The Declaration speaks of the "right to welfare and employment." The Chinese take this as a basic right—in contrast to the frequent attitude in Western society that welfare or social security is a gift that one part of society (the good guys) gives to the other part.

Medical care is listed as a right in the sense that all should be able to afford it. In China the approach is that health care is a right requiring only minimal fees which anyone can afford. This, in fact, is a good area in which to see the tension between the rights of individuals and collective rights. What do you do if doctors don't want to work in remote areas? Or if there is a brain drain and your doctors want to go to another country where they can earn more money?

In China there is great social pressure for doctors to go to rural areas where the majority of the people live. It is difficult to leave China. Is this a violation of the rights of doctors? Or does it meet the right of the people to have health care?

Alan Geyer, former editor of *Christian Century*, has visited China and reflects on human rights there in the context of medical care:

> I speak of the right to life in a much broader sense: the right of the human being to the security of her or his physical and mental existence, in a society committed to a healthful environment and to the provision of adequate care for every sick or injured person, regardless of social or economic circumstances. . . . The Chinese have essentially solved the problem of the vindication of human rights in their health care system. I can document that assertion, for everyone I know who has studied Chinese health care, or has seen it in operation, or has been a patient in it, agrees that it is one of the most remarkable human achievements of any society in this century. . . .
>
> This poorest of societies has, in one generation, so organized its training of health professionals and paraprofessionals, and its network of health services, that basic health security has become a matter both of human right and physical reality—for virtually everyone in China. . . . .
>
> The achievement of the Chinese people in health care is a challenge to our own definitions of human rights and our own [American] health care priorities. The discrepancy between the mythology about medical care in this country and the empirical reality needs to be confronted. . . .
>
> In short, . . . revolution has promoted an immense program of human welfare, dignity, and self-respect—perhaps laying the foundation for what will eventually be a more human approach to civil liberties and political participation. . . .
>
> Having both [medical] training and delivery directed by clear norms of social justice is, of course, in sharp contrast with the United States' continuing style of individualistic entrepreneurship. A Chinese who is a high official in the World Health Organization was recently asked what the most important qualification for doctors in China is. Without hesitation he replied: "Compassion." That reply is echoed by Chiu Chia-Hsiang, an official of the Shanghai Second Medical School, who says: 'The social conscience of the student is so elevated that he puts the public needs ahead of his own. If there is a locality with an urgent

need for a surgeon, then he might go on to become one. But he could
happily go on to become an internist instead, if he were so needed."

. . . I do not want to fall into the trap of comparing an idealized view
of Chinese health care with a cynical view of American health care. . . .
[Stories from China do] not warrant the generalization that all Chinese
doctors and hospital workers are compassionate, while all American
doctors and hospitals are inhumane. But I do not retreat from my
primary position that the right to life has yet to be vindicated in the
American health-care system while the Chinese have essentially vindicated that right in their system. . . .

The issue of human rights is complex and generalization always dangerous. Nevertheless, in what Alan Geyer has said in the preceding paragraphs
and in the quotation that follows, points are made about human rights
which are worthy of our consideration.

Two Americans from Detroit, after extensive travel in China, wrote:

Whether you agree or disagree with their conclusions, the people of
China believe they are free. They believe they enjoy a type of democracy and freedom which protects their fundamental rights.

In terms of international relations, they believe China is running its
own affairs for the first time in over a century. In terms of internal
affairs, they believe the people of China are controlling their own lives
for the first time in history.

Are they brainwashed? Fooled? Intimidated?

We returned home with the inescapable conclusion that they believed
these things because their new system has delivered. The average person, the peasant and the worker, has for the first time in memory been
able to:

    —eat, not starve
    —build a home, not wander about in poverty
    —wear decent clothes, not rags
    —enjoy family life, not sell children into brothels and slavery
    —read, not depend on rich scholars for knowledge
    —voice their opinions, not lose their heads for speaking out
    —and build the kind of society these basics imply.

They paid for these changes with their blood. However we may judge it,
they were determined to protect and preserve their new order.

They did not define their democracy and freedom in abstract, intellectual terms. They simply looked at their own lives, past and present.

Basic to the Chinese transformation of society has been the continuing
quest to eliminate special privileges for those with more education, wealth,

or responsibility. Some observers have expressed admiration for the Chinese achievement of a more egalitarian society but regret the existence of compulsory political education and political movements. In the following passage George and Jennie Ling report on this topic.

Political education and political movements are necessarily part and parcel of the Chinese system. Since there is no money incentive, such movements are the driving force for effective work. They are designed to change people's perspectives and values so that people assume responsibility for social problems, find fulfilment in collective effort and take pride in communal success. They attempt to reinforce social justice by checking abuses of privilege.

In our ten years in China we witnessed at least five major campaigns. Yet no one lost a job at the local level. Unless the person was guilty of a felony punishable by law, the usual penalty of transgression was a warning and the writing of a self-criticism. The public to which one addressed the self-criticism depended on the number of people affected by one's mistake. In a factory, if one's action affected only one's small work group, self-criticism would be given only to the work group; if factory-wide, to a factory meeting. If the head of a city was found to have abused privilege, the whole city would hear his self-criticism by radio.

What about the protection of individual rights in this process? When there are wrongs, channels for rectification exist. For example, during the early part of the Cultural Revolution, our family's home was searched by Red Guards and some things considered to be "bourgeois" taken away. This kind of a search without warrant is contrary to Party policy. After an investigation, all the things taken away were returned. Any missing items were remunerated with cash.

Another case. Our factory, together with another factory, ran a high school. One of our factory's workers served as a part-time teacher in the school. After a strong disagreement with the school leader, this teacher was arrested. It was said he had committed a wrong against a girl student. Several weeks passed and still the teacher was detained. Someone in our factory put up a poster demanding to know the facts of the case against this teacher. More posters went up. Finally the teacher was released and cleared of any charges.

Now, this is a sad case, indicating injustices that do occur. On the other hand, it serves as an illustration of how injustices are checked. The workers were responsible enough to demand the protection of the human rights of a fellow worker.

Checks on the abuses of privilege are enforced by generally accepted norms. In China, these norms are the Party policies and discipline. Chinese leadership policies have not just "appeared." They grow up through the history of the Chinese Communist Party and are the undergirding and binding force in Chinese society much like the Constitution is to Americans or common law to the British. When policies are trespassed, as does occasionally occur, Marxist values, as made concrete by Party policies and discipline, become the criteria of evaluation. Political movements are the occasions in which people's dedication, moral character, and actual deeds come under evaluation.

Certainly China has not solved the problem of inequality. But as long as special privileges are considered abnormalities, as long as there are effective means to check these abnormalities, the situation is encouraging. Since the Cultural Revolution it is clear that the danger of social injustice comes not so much from ordinary people but from the corruption of high officials within the Party. People now have more opportunity to ask the authorities questions and to be critical of the Party. Many more documents from the central government are read and vigorously debated at the grass-roots level.

The voice of the people is taken more seriously by authorities. The right to strike and write wall posters, included in the new constitution (1974), give people new opportunities to express their views.

During and after the Cultural Revolution we saw inexperienced cadres seek privileges such as an unfair allocation of scarce commodities or using influence to get children into college. When political movement occurred, these transgressions of Party policies were judged. Some might be cunning enough to escape one movement, but there would be a second, a third. . . .

In summary, in the fewer than 30 years China has been liberated, priority has gone to building up the new social and economic base. As the system has matured and gained confidence in its social, political and economic achievements, more attention has been given to human rights. People are given the right to voice disagreement with government decisions in a way that was not possible in earlier days.

We know several instances in which workers resisted a government policy by slowing down in their work or not showing up for work if the policy was not in their interests. The government did not penalize the workers. The workers even continued to draw salary. This would have been unthinkable during the formative years of the People's Republic when such workers might have been penalized for sabotage. Today people in leadership positions are more likely to patiently explain the rationale

behind policies and try to persuade workers that they are in their best interests.

This chapter has looked at several goals of community life in China—its demands for social responsibility, its attempt to allocate human resources in a way that is fair, yet allows for creativity. We have considered the Chinese view of human rights and political campaigns as a means of struggling against inequities that continue to exist.

Apparently many Chinese find fulfillment in their community-oriented society. Questioning the capitalist system is considered near heresy for most North Americans. Yet China's attempt to create a system without economic competition warrants our attention.

Information about China continues, of course, to be limited. In a country of China's size incidents which support other interpretations will happen. Undoubtedly violations of human rights do occur. That the Gang of Four (see page 22), at the time of this writing still under criticism for restrictive policies, could attain power shows that there are weaknesses in the Chinese system that remain to be overcome. Yet the Chinese attempt to balance community and individual needs is important for us to watch.

The late Premier Chou En-lai, in conversation with an American visitor, commented that the Cultural Revolution slogan "all public, no self," used to justify extreme suppression of individuality, is wrong. Nor is "all self, no public" correct. A balance between public and self is essential.

It may be that China can be faulted for too much emphasis on community. But when we do fault it, we need to look with equal rigor at our own society's individualistic orientation. Chou En-lai is undoubtedly right —the solution is neither "all public" nor "all self." How do we maintain a healthy tension between the two?

IV

THE HUMAN DIMENSION

by Donald E. MacInnis

As we begin the long plane descent across central China from the west, the landscape comes into focus. Tiny villages come into view dotting the Yangtze valley plain. I quickly count 50 villages, dark, not a light showing, no movement of cars on highways, no red glow from taillights or shopping plazas—no highways; the only mark of modernity the ruler-straight scribe of a railroad cutting eastward through the rice fields. Wisps of smoke begin to drift upward from the villages. The people who live there are making small kitchen fires with straw, twigs, coal balls, preparing breakfast. What do they think if they glance upward at the giant plane from Paris—from outer space? What do they think as they plan their day, their week, their lives? Have we anything in common?

In September 1974 I visited a collective farm near Nanking bordering the Yangtze River. An older farm couple, the Wangs, invited a few of us into their two-room brick house recently built by the man and his sons. He was proud of it; he owns it and can leave it upon his death to his children.

The courtyard, no larger than half a volleyball court, was crammed with growing things: garlic, pole beans, cabbage, mustard greens, tobacco, rabbits, chickens, a fat black pig. We would call the home austere, even primitive. A bare bulb hung from the ceiling in each room. Water came from a well and pump outside the kitchen door. The furniture was simple —chairs, table, beds, small radio, clock, kitchen utensils, a blanket chest. No refrigerator, no washer or dryer, no shower or bathtub. Family snapshots were grouped on a wall.

What, we asked Mr. Wang, is the difference between life now and life in old China? His face blackened by the sun and lined by years of labor, accented by cropped gray hair and a grizzle of whiskers, Mr. Wang summed up his answer in a short phrase: "Personal security for myself and my family." He explained what he meant.

"In old China we had nothing; we were at the mercy of fate, the weather, the landlord, the moneylender, the local war lord and his bandit-soldiers. There was no government. We had no security. When the landlord threw us off the land we had nothing to do but beg. My sister was taken by the landlord; the rest of us became beggars. After Liberation we got a piece of land. Later we pooled our tools and labor with other farmers and formed a mutual aid team. Finally we pooled our land and formed the New Life People's Commune. Today 20,600 people in 5,060 families live here. There are 960 hectares of land divided among 85 work teams. We raise vegetables, rice and pigs. We no longer haul water from the river." (He gestured at the pump.)

Mr. Wang described the crops, the new irrigation system, the small industries for processing grain, making coarse paper from straw, noodle-making; the schools, the medical clinics, and the campaigns to eliminate the "four pests"—flies, rats, bedbugs, and mosquitoes. Malaria is no longer endemic in this wetland rice area. As for his own family, "We now have personal security, something we never had before." What did he mean by that?

"In the old society I had no job security. The landlord could throw me off the land as he wished. We never knew if we would eat the next meal or not. We had no health security. If I became ill, or hurt myself at work, I would have no place for medical care. There was no real doctor, and I couldn't afford the herb doctor. My children would have no education. The most I could hope is to apprentice them to an artisan or shopkeeper, at no pay at all until they learned the trade. We had no old age security, other than what our children might provide. Today, if we don't stay with our children, we can live in a Home for Respected Persons on a small pension. We have a cooperative health care system which covers our whole family. The county has a proper hospital and doctors. Our children can all get a basic education, even the girls; our oldest girl went on to a teacher training college and now she's a teacher. As for food, clothing and shelter, if for some reason this job should be closed to me, I would be guaranteed another job. That's the difference between China before and after Liberation for us."

THE HUMAN CONDITION

While agriculture, technology and science research are areas of concern and development in China, the central phenomenon is people. More than 10 billion human beings have lived and struggled for survival across the face of China; nearly one billion of those are alive today, and most of them live in the grain-growing eastern provinces, perhaps 85 percent of 900 million people crammed into an area equivalent to the United States east of the Mississippi River. A thousand generations have left their mark on the land, society, and culture of the world's oldest surviving civilization. Fourteen million new births add to this present generation each year. Few landscapes are more human. In China it is still men and women, not machines, who plant, cultivate and harvest the crops. Farming in China is more like gardening; the soil is cherished, nothing is wasted.

A Minnesota farmer in 1976 visited farms in various parts of China. His observation: the corn, wheat, and soybean yields are as high as ours, "but they put an awful lot of labor into those crops. They virtually plant and weed those crops by hand. It takes 80 percent of their people to raise those crops, while we do it with 4 percent of ours and export a surplus to boot."

A western Canadian farmer comments, "I used to feel superior because I planted and harvested more land. After seeing how Chinese farmers support so many people on such little acreage, I think differently. Maybe that's more important."

The central fact in China is people. Chairman Mao knew that; it was his belief in people—the workers and peasants—that galvanized the forces of opposition to the old society. Billboards, posters, comic books emulating heroes, films, revolutionary operas, poems all affirm this faith in the people: "The people alone are the motive force in history."

The ideology is materialistic; that is, they find truth only in material values susceptible to objective and scientific testing, rejecting metaphysical, spiritual, and idealist concepts. Mao Tse-tung, a sensitive poet, often called a "revolutionary romantic," was eminently practical in day-to-day tactics. He once wrote, "We stand for self-reliance. . . . We depend on our own efforts, on the creative power of the entire people." He believed that the future of China was in the hands of the working class—the workers and peasants. "If they take their destiny into their own hands [and] take an active attitude in solving problems instead of evading them, there will be no difficulty in the world which they cannot overcome."

This sounds very much like the North American no-nonsense spirit of getting a job done. Perhaps that is why we are so fascinated by China. We see a situation that short years ago seemed hopeless but today is dramatically reversed. We are haunted by the specter of impending catastrophe as the graph lines of global population growth and food production intersect. The West has abandoned the Enlightenment belief in progress and moral perfectibility and despairs over the persistence of global inflation, poverty, hunger, despoliation of resources, environmental overload, wars, racial conflicts, and inequities in ownership of wealth.

In China, we see a people that appear to be coping successfully with these and other problems that plague the nations of the world. Travelling in China one sees a healthy people, no signs of malnutrition, no scrawny mothers with their starving babies begging for pennies or a handful of rice. Perhaps it is the healthy children, eyes clear of trachoma, skin free of ringworm and scabies, no sign of rickets, bloat or parasitic infestation, that are most impressive. Their parents—workers and peasants—go about their work with quiet dignity, showing a sense of self-worth and pride by the way they look the visitor in the eye and respond to questions as equals.

A SECULAR HUMANISM

China may be the most secular society in the world today—secular defined as this-worldly, temporal, human-centered. In cities, towns, and villages marked by thousands of temples, shrines, monasteries, pagodas, and churches, all but a few of these buildings now appear to be abandoned or converted to secular purposes.

The Confucianist will say that the Chinese were never a religious people. The Chinese, of all the world's cultures, are unique in having no creation myth; they have regarded the world and man as uncreated, existing spontaneously in a cosmos with no external cause or authority. Joseph Needham, the British scholar, calls the Chinese cosmic model "an ordered harmony of wills without an ordainer."

The Maoist worldview, equally secular, sees creation as an ongoing, dialectical, human-centered process, by and for the people. Confucianism was a secular humanism—the most unequivocal the world has known, because it found the source and measure of values in humankind alone. If there is a Heaven (and Confucius did not rule out that possibility, although he remained a skeptic to the end), then Heaven too is made in the measure of humanity's vision. The Mandate of Heaven in fact meant the Mandate of the People: when the ruler had failed his task, he lost the Mandate and the people rebelled. Mencius, by saying, "Heaven hears as the people hear; heaven sees as the people see," affirmed the people as both the source of judgment for government and the standard for heaven itself. These words of Mencius are echoed in Mao's "Foolish Old Man" essay discussed in Chapter One, "Our God is none other than the Chinese people."

China's secularism is a humanism in direct line with the Confucian heritage—although today's leaders deny this fact. Mao Tse-tung and his generation were educated traditionally, steeped in the classics. Humanism, defined as any system of thought or action in which human values, interests, and dignity predominate, characterized Confucianism as it does the system of Mao Tse-tung. But China's secularism today does not imitate or resemble the atomistic model of *The Secular City* of the 1960's. On the contrary, the people of China's cities and villages find no escape from each other. In a nation approaching one billion in number, the problems of providing basic material needs for daily living and sheer survival demand collective action; there is no place for the Taoist hermit or the lonely eccentric.

Maoism, like Confucianism, is characterized by social responsibility, personal ethics, and a rational approach to solving problems and needs of daily living. Unlike Confucianism, the dominant class in China today is the working class, and the goal is social egalitarianism rather than a stratified hierarchy with an educated elite in control of wealth and power. Moreover, in contrast to the Confucian belief in harmony and the Golden Mean as a supreme virtue, Mao Tse-tung elevates struggle to that position: struggle against traditional class inequities, against fate, against nature itself.

The people of China today project a spirit of determination and self-reliance, exemplified by the model Tachai Brigade. "In Agriculture Study Tachai" is the slogan seen everywhere on billboards and posters throughout China. Using nothing but hand tools and their own brute labor, Tachai Brigade, with fewer than 100 families, transformed a barren tract of rocky, eroded hillsides and gullies into a productive model farm. The message is clear: there can be a secure living standard for everyone in China. Even seemingly hopeless land can be salvaged and transformed, but not by some outside benefactor; it requires sacrifice, deferred gratification, collective hard work.

DON'T RELY ON HEAVEN

This spirit of purpose, future-oriented in contrast to the Confucian longing for a lost Golden Age, is based in the experience of a revolution won against seemingly hopeless odds. There is a Promethean mystique that literally challenges the gods. China's posters, painted in vivid colors by worker-artists, show men and women working in teams, conquering every kind of hardship in building a new nation and a better life. Strong, healthy, smiling, larger than life, they are living proof that anything is possible; never again (these posters say) will workers and peasants be downtrodden, hungry, abandoned, sick, and in misery.

One of these posters, painted by peasant artists from a North China collective farm, is titled *Bu Kao Tien*, "Don't Rely on Heaven!" The scene is traditional in Chinese art: rugged mountains, tumbling streams, verdant nature, people. But people, unlike the Taoist landscapes with their meditative scholars, are no longer dwarfed by nature; on the contrary, men and women, collectively, have remade nature.

The vaulting slopes are terraced from top to bottom, the stream is harnessed by a dam, high voltage lines bring power to a whitewashed pumphouse and water gushes from hand-held hoses onto the topmost planted terrace. Thirty-nine peasants in eight separate work teams irrigate, spray, cultivate, and work the fields. Fruit trees blossom in a riot of color. A red tractor, made in China, towing a load rounds the corner on a tree-lined road. "Overcome Heaven Bridge" crosses the diked canal, and a poster on the pumphouse wall declares, "People Will Surely Overcome Heaven."

But *Bu Kao Tien*, "Don't Rely on Heaven," is not meant to be anti-religious; rather it is pro-humanity. "The people, and the people alone, are the motive force in history."

Tien means heaven; it also refers to nature, sky, the source of rain; and it can mean fate as well. *Bu Kao Tien* in this poster means, "Don't wait for flood or drought to ruin your crops and starve your children. Take fate into your own hands. Working together we can have this kind [as in the poster] of heaven here on earth."

The intended message is positive; the poster celebrates the liberation of the Chinese peasants from poverty and suffering through their own

collective efforts, liberation from tradition, passivity, superstition, hopelessness, and exploitation.
There is a new spirit in today's China. The changes are overwhelming to one who lived in China before. They have been reported many times by visitors, scholars, journalists: no beggars, no homeless street-sleepers, no drug abuse, no pornography, no exploitation of sex and violence in the public media, no alienated subculture driven to street crime and delinquency. By all evidence there is no black market, no government corruption, and there is a social discipline that is hard to find in the West. The Chinese family system is alive and well—often three generations live comfortably together; the divorce rate is minuscule, and venereal disease and illegitimacy are virtually unknown. There is full employment, adequate food in the markets, no inflation in consumer prices, and an impressive 7 percent annual growth rate in the economy. At the same time there is no freedom to publish a *Playboy* or *Ramparts* magazine, to open a private shop or business, or to escape the law with the help of lawyers.

RELIGION IN CHINA TODAY

Confucianism was a system of humanistic ethics in a human-centered world, but Confucius was not irreligious. By his time the ancestral cult, both for families and the state, was firmly established. Instructing people on how to participate in family and state rites, he urged a spirit of reverence, *"as if* the spirits were present." Whether there are spirits present or not, the attitude of reverence is to be assumed "as if" they were. And this indeed was the practice in all Chinese families down to this generation. Even Christians maintained the genealogical records and ancestral tablets with scrupulous fidelity.

One seldom sees the old-style graves in the open fields of China today. Graves from a thousand generations once occupied precious cropland; in recent years the land was cleared, the bones placed in urns, or (if long abandoned) powdered and scattered. Burial in hillside graves is still common in rural areas, while in cities cremation is the usual mode. What of the ancestor cult? The ancestor tablets, once the central shrine and sacred tie binding every family-clan, are gone now. There is a larger loyalty; Mao saw the authority of the clan system and the ancestral temple as one of the "four thick ropes" binding the Chinese people, particularly the peasants. The other three were the authority of the political system, the supernatural (religious) system "ranging from the King of Hell down to the town and village gods," and the domination of women by men.

Mao Tse-tung's view of religion, in my opinion, is that of a Confucian secularist, conditioned by his reading of Marx and Engels and his negative impressions of village Buddhism and local cult religions gained when he was a child and youth. In an early essay on dialectical materialism he expounds the Marxist view that primitive people, unable to explain the phenomena of natural forces, "sought help from spirits. This is the origin of religion and idealism." But as the people learned to harness the forces of nature for productive uses, they came to see "the futility of the illusions of religion and idealism and to arrive at materialist conclusions."

In a long interview in 1965 with Andre Malraux, the late French Minister of Culture, Mao gave this personal statement of faith.

> When I said, "Chinese Marxism is the religion of the people," I meant that the Communists express the Chinese people in a real way if they remain faithful to the work upon which the whole of China has embarked as if on another Long March. When we say, "We are the Sons of People," China understands it as she understood the phrase "Son of Heaven." The People has taken the place of the ancestors. The People, not the victorious Communist party.

Malraux closes the account with a slogan from earlier days of guerrilla warfare: "Gods are all right for the rich; the poor have the Eighth Route Army."

As in so many other policy issues, in his attitude toward religion Mao Tse-tung was a voluntarist, opposed to coercion. In his landmark essay *On the Correct Handling of Contradictions* (1957) he wrote:

> We cannot abolish religion by administrative decree or force people not to believe in it. . . . The only way to settle questions of an ideological nature or controversial issues among the people is by the democratic method, the method of discussion, of criticism, of persuasion and education, and not by the method of coercion or repression.

Religion is simply bypassed, left behind in the headlong rush of socialist nation-building and cultural revolution. The view that religion is an outdated relic carried over from primitive societies ignorant of the laws of science and nature is taught in the schools. Yet "freedom of religious belief" is guaranteed in the Constitution, and groups of Christians, Moslems, and Buddhists continue to meet together for worship and fellowship in the villages and neighborhoods of China. Past years have seen periods of local repression and hardship for religious believers, but current reports indicate that Christians and other believers quietly but openly practice their faith.

For China's secularized society today religion is not a threat; it's simply irrelevant. During a visit to the Nanking Teachers College, I talked with a young woman student about religion.

I had seen books on religion, biblical theology, Christian history and philosophy on the open shelves of the college library—none checked out since the late 1940's. As we crossed the lush green landscaped campus warmed by the September sun I asked her: "Do you or any of your friends believe in Christianity or the traditional religions of China?"

Her reply snapped back: "There's no need for that. With the basis of scientific materialism of the new society, the old superstitions were proved to be false. Only old people, if any, are seen worshipping in the temples."

"Is it not true," I asked, "that China's youth learn a great deal by discussing the former days with older people? Could they not learn something by discussing religion with their elders?"

"Why would anyone want to discuss religion?" she replied. "What does that have to do with our new society? It simply would not interest young people. It's irrelevant."

"Of course," she added, "our people have freedom of religious belief; it's guaranteed by our Constitution. The Chinese people also have the right not to believe, and the right to propagate atheism."

Religion was in decline in China long before the founding of the Chinese Communist Party in 1921. Hundreds of anti-Christian incidents in the nineteenth and twentieth centuries were due more to the endemic antiforeignism generated by the privileged position of all foreigners under the "unequal treaties" imposed after the Opium War (1839-42) than to hostility to religion. Apathy and lack of interest caused widespread attrition of China's traditional religions during the modernizing period. Modern education and exposure to ideas from the West brought a new generation of youth and leaders who found no answers for China's needs in temples and sutras.

Christianity, for some of the educated patriots, seemed to be the source of creative energy that drove the West. Educated in mission schools and colleges, influenced by the YMCA/YWCA, returned from study in Christian schools abroad, or touched in other ways by the Christian church and mission, many of them became leaders in China's political and social revival prior to the anti-Japanese war. But the tensions generated by the forces of secularization, modernization, and nationalism worked against all religions, including Christianity. The anti-religious movement concurrent with Chiang Kai-shek's Northern Expedition (1925-26), fueled by the anti-foreignism of that period, focused particularly on Christianity. Later, China's millions were too deeply involved in the anti-Japanese war and civil turmoil to support any major religious movement. In 1949 no more than 1 percent of China's people were Christians. By 1952 the missionaries had left China; none has yet returned except as a visitor.

Since 1949 Buddhists, Christians, and Moslems maintained public worship but with increasing restrictions and controls as the years passed. According to reports, all surviving public places of religious activity were closed in 1966 by roving bands of young Red Guards at the start of the Cultural Revolution. Although religion was not mentioned as a target in the Cultural Revolution directives, the Red Guards assumed it belonged to the "Four Olds" (old habits, ideas, customs, and culture) and attempted to erase the religious heritage along with other aspects of the old society. Temples, mosques, and churches were damaged and sacred books were burned. Some such actions have since been criticized as not in accord with proper policies. It was not until 1972 that visitors reported two churches in Peking opened once again for worshippers from the foreign community.

Subsequent reports from overseas Chinese visitors indicate that small numbers of Christians meet regularly and openly in villages and neighborhoods for worship and Bible study. These "house church" groups meet in homes and public meeting rooms, but not in the foreign-style churches which carry a stigma from the former colonial days.

THE FUTURE: A PERSONAL STATEMENT

What of the future? One can assume that the leadership of China will hold to its present policy of self-reliance, declining all offers of aid assistance from mission societies, Peace Corps volunteers, United Nations agencies and other persons or groups bearing gifts and services. Chinese government representatives in Peking and foreign capitals politely declined offers of help at the time of the earthquake disaster in Tangshan in the summer of 1976. Liberated from a century of humiliating foreign incursions and dependence, the Chinese will not easily surrender their present self-sufficiency.

Yet any secular system, in my opinion, no matter how successful in organizing a just society and elevating public morality, is impoverished if it lacks a deep and comprehensive religious vision. Throughout history men and women everywhere have searched for ultimate meaning beyond the immediate and tangible. The individual's moral and intellectual quest finally meets a cutoff point, I feel, a void which cannot be bridged without a religious vision.

The seeds of China's church of the future probably will be found in the Christians who maintain their faith and practice in China today. Through their experience and witness the Christian message may be made relevant to a people conditioned to materialist values and secularist teaching.

I see Christianity as a teaching, a faith system, an understanding of the human condition under divine grace that offers hope, both for life on earth and life hereafter. The witness of the church in China, I would say, has had a double mandate, *kerygma* and *diakonia,* that is, evangelism and service: to "make disciples of all nations, baptizing them in the name of the Father, Son and Holy Spirit"; and to bring "release to the captives, recovering of sight to the blind, to set at liberty those who are oppressed, and to proclaim the acceptable year of the Lord." In my opinion, China's Christians, and those everywhere, if they are to serve as the salt and leaven of society, must practice the kind of self-giving responsiveness to divine grace which manifests a personal liberation that both comprises and transcends the liberation offered by secular systems.

ODE TO THE PLUM BLOSSOM

December 1961

Wind and rain escorted Spring's departure,
Flying snow welcomes Spring's return.
On the ice-clad rock rising high and sheer
A flower blooms sweet and fair.

Sweet and fair, she craves not Spring for herself alone,
To be the harbinger of Spring she is content.
When the mountain flowers are in full bloom
She will smile mingling in their midst.

Mao Tse-tung

V
CHRIST AND COMMUNITY IN NEW CHINA

Donald MacInnis' personal statement about the future of Christianity in China, which concluded the previous chapter, brings us into this chapter's subject. How are we, as Christians, to respond to the vast, complex, and controversial questions which China raises for us? How can we put the China event into a framework which makes sense for us in the church? What have we learned to help us in our search for community?

In order to approach these questions we have brought together here a number of different Christian views on China. We will first quote the words of Chinese Christian K. H. Ting and his wife Siu-mei. He is president of Nanking Theological College, and she teaches at Nanking University. Questions were put to them by a delegation including Fugene L. Stockwell which visited Nanking in 1976; Dr. Stockwell prepared the text of the conversation reproduced below.

The Tings make three points especially important in the context of this book. First, they do not expect the churches in China to play an active role in international ecumenical study and conferences. This fact means that the task of seeking the significance of China's experience for our search for community will fall to Christians outside China. Second, they point out the relationship between missions and Western power as a reason for Chinese people's loss of interest in Christianity. Another reason for church decline is that many of the physical and spiritual needs which led people into the church have been met in the new political situation. It is not because of pressure from the government but because of these other historical and social factors that few people are attracted to Christianity, according to the Tings. Thirdly, the Tings feel that God is working in socialist China, and that for 2,000 years Christians have been able to appreciate good things that happen outside the church.

Following the Ting interview we outline some of the responses of Christians outside China to the China experience.

A CHINESE CHRISTIAN VIEW OF CHINA

Question: What is the place of Christianity in this society?

K.H. Ting: That question cannot be isolated from a previous question: What has been the place of Christianity in the past? The main influx of Protestant and Roman Catholic missionaries was in the 19th and 20th centuries. Individual missionaries may be quite innocent, but the missionary movement was part of a system. Missionaries were tools of imperialist aggression. We have strong views on this point. We do not think the missionary movement contributed to the liberation of the Chinese people. Indeed, it worked against our revolution in many ways. Christianity has never been a popular religion in China, even though there were more missionaries here than anywhere else. The number of converts was very small. Even today Chinese Christians have to live down that past association. Christianity has always been something foreign to China. It was not rejected before liberation because of military support from imperialist states. After liberation this situation was different. The Chinese people were angry with missionaries and churches. Many buildings had been built with money paid as indemnity for missionary lawsuits. Missionaries called in gunboats to enforce certain policies, and Chinese officers would get money from ordinary people—and that money was used to build churches. When *you* see a church you see something holy, but to many Chinese a church is a reminder of the imperialist past. . . .

Question: What is the role of the Religious Affairs Bureau in Peking?

K.H. Ting: Through it we are exempted from paying taxes on land. When some students wanted to study in the seminary, the Bureau would help see to it that they would not have other work. No indication was given as to study content.

In the past Nanking Seminary was like colleges in the US, but Chinese society has changed tremendously. Our Christian groups are very small. They are scattered. There are few Christian groups that still have paid clergy. We cannot afford to maintain salaried ministers. With the new esteem in which labor is held, many of our ministers have wanted to identify themselves with the workers around them. They feel they do not want to be full-time ministers. Our Protestant Christianity is declergyized, deinstitutionalized. We do not have denominations. Ours is a postdenominational Christianity. Christians meet informally in homes or in any room they can borrow. They do not use church buildings. Part of the reason is financial—we cannot maintain them. Nanking once had 35 church buildings for 500 Protestants; they were attracted here because Nanking was Chiang Kai-shek's capital. We saw no point in maintaining these buildings; especially since the Cultural Revolution, Chinese Christians have not wanted to use them.

Given this situation, it is unthinkable to maintain a five-year course for students to educate them in an ivory tower to be a new elite. Christians will not support them anyway. I wonder if we would be able to get worthy young people in socialist China. We have some short-term training courses as experiments. We want to know what sort of theological education would be consonant with the new China. A certain amount of theological education can be sent to where the people are.

There is a constant decrease in the number of Christians. The Chinese have never been very religious. In the past, people went into religion mainly because of suffering. They wanted to get medical help, education, support. This drew them into the churches. Another reason for people to be religious in those days was the disharmony among families. In the new China the life of the people has improved a great deal. No one needs to worry about starvation, medical help, etc. That part of the Christian church's attraction no longer exists. Human relationships have not entirely changed, but they do not seem to bring about great pessimism and frustration. Given the imperialist background, it is understandable that the number of believers would decline. There have been new converts, but the number is not large.

Question: Would you agree that Christianity will die out in China when today's Christians die?

K.H. Ting: I would not be too surprised if that were to be the case, but I think that there are bound to be people, if in small numbers, who with all their political enthusiasm will still believe that it is Christian faith and teaching that will give them answers about ultimate questions. A Christianity which has divested itself of harmful background things can satisfy the needs of these people. But such people will be few. I do not foresee the evangelization of all or even half of China. Protestants are about one-tenth of 1 percent of the population. This has nothing to do with the Communist Party's policy on religion. The right to hold religious beliefs is to be respected. The party thinks that religion itself is bad, but building up socialist China is a task for all people who can be united in it—and is more important than struggling against religious faith. In the united front we say that we are to seek our common ground—opposition to imperialism and feudalism, for example. This is more important than maintaining our differences, as for instance over the question whether there is a God. The Chinese Communists are very anxious that Christians be within the united front.

We returned to China in 1951. People in Europe were very concerned about our coming back. They felt I would be killed or put in a concentration camp. I am still alive, and I do not believe that there is any such camp. We do not need it. I have been engaged in religious work all these years. I believe in the honesty of the Communists concerning the policy of religious freedom. But not everything needs to be kept intact as it was 27 years ago.

Question: What about the relationship between Chinese Christians and Christians in other Third World countries?
K.H. Ting: Some Christians think about this, others do not. In the West sometimes it is said that Chinese Christians are not permitted to come into contact with any foreign visitors except those who are approved by the regime. . . .

Some Chinese Christians are angry about these matters. Others think that in principle there is no objection [to meeting with foreign Christians] and that such contact may be beneficial.

But I think we must not expend much time and energy in maintaining international contacts, or in going to many meetings abroad. Our situation in China is entirely different from that in other places. For example, we are not interested in women's ordination . . . because we have discarded ordination entirely. We think many of these international gatherings are becoming places where the Soviet Union and the US contend with each other. The World Council of Churches is such a place. The US and the USSR cooperate when the goals are common; they contend when their goals differ.

Question: Do not First and Third World Christians need to be more aware of the Chinese Christian experience? How do we learn from you?

K.H. Ting: An analogy is the protective tariff. We are trying to make Christianity Chinese. We cannot afford to be inundated by Western or African things. We must raise our barriers. Later we can lower our tariff. . . .

Question: What is the place of the Holy Spirit here? Has it left the church because the church did such a bad job? Is it working in disguise through Marxism in China? Do Chinese get along well without dealing with the ultimate questions?

Siu-Mei Ting: As Chinese Christians we do not see Christianity and socialist China as opposed to each other. It is God working, whether in his name or not. We do not pose the question this way.

K.H. Ting: This question does not need to be raised with China only. For 2,000 years the Christian church has faced the question of how to account for things that are good and beautiful which are found outside the churches. Very few Christians would say that all these things are done by the devil in the garb of an angel. Christians have always appreciated good things that have appeared outside the churches, in science and in art. What is happening in China is only one of these things, on a larger scale. Christianity is not something political and socialism is not something theological, though outside there are discussions about the theological implications of the new China. China has not posed a new theological problem for the church. . . .

Question: What is happening to worshiping groups of Christians? What about Bible study?

K.H. Ting: Christianity in China is more and more a world view in the minds of those who still hold to the truth of the Bible. It is mainly a world view, not an institution. We have done away with institutions and church buildings. There is a very informal relation among Christians. They meet very informally, not even on Sunday mornings because factories are open on Sundays. Mostly Christians meet in the evenings, not necessarily every week, maybe once every two or three weeks, as they decide. They just meet as Christians. There is no ritual. They share their convictions or insights after studying the Bible or after certain experiences. The Quakers would feel at home. We do study the Bible. Our meetings are very simple, just meetings. . . .

The implications of the Chinese experience for our understanding of community life and Christian mission appear differently to different people. Somewhat arbitrarily we divide these responses into our four groups. These groupings are not mutually exclusive, and the same person may fit into more than one.

First, the "Visible Church" approach affirms the primary and present role of the Christian community in China in achieving or assuring fullness of life. Verbal evangelism is therefore given high priority. Second, the "Lord of History" approach finds God's saving grace mediated through non-Christian as well as Christian persons and events and even sees signs of salvation in Mao's China. Third, the "Values" approach emphasizes the Christian dimension of Mao's values. Fourth, the "Mirror" approach seeks to re-define mission theology in light of China's experience and sees China as counterfoil, a positive but alien experience, through which we can see ourselves more clearly. We shall now look more closely at each of these four types and give examples of each.

THE "VISIBLE CHURCH" APPROACH

Those who take this path affirm the need for verbal evangelization of the people of China. Most significant for them are not stories of the changes brought about in China through the people's struggle to overcome oppression but stories of continued church activity in China. Some are content to leave the task of evangelism to Christians in China. Others see the need to mount a new "mission offensive" in China, although they might be split over the question of whether this should be a Western undertaking or a Third World Christian responsibility or an exclusive prerogative of overseas Chinese Christians. Others caution patience but still look to an eventual effort to incorporate more of the Chinese people into the church. This view often goes hand in hand with a negative assessment of revolutionary culture in China but not necessarily.

A pamphlet by Jonathan Chao, "The Spirit of God at Work in China," presents one variation of this approach.

In the recent (1975) Chinese Christian Students Summer Conference. . . I was asked to conduct a workshop on "Our Tasks Today for the Future Evangelization of China." Part of the workshop was an interview with two young people who came out of China recently. . . .

Q: When did you leave Mainland China?
A: I left China in July 1973.

Q: Are there Christians in your village?
A: Yes, there are, but only six families.

Q: How about your neighboring villages?
A: . . . In another village . . . there are many Christians. In fact, it has the largest number of Christians in our whole country. About 30 percent are Christians. . . .

Q: How did it happen that an entire production brigade turned Christian?

A: In that particular production brigade there were two or three families who were unusually zealous for the Lord. They were really willing to put themselves wholly unto prayer for the salvation of the entire production brigade. They helped everyone who needed help. Non-Christians in that village were exceedingly moved. They felt that it was great to be Christians. So they, too, believed in the Lord. Another important reason is that wherever Christians are active, the devil is also extremely active. At one time there were many in that village who were possessed by demons. Not a few were mentally sick, too. So all the Christians prayed for them, and they were healed, and the demons were expelled. . . .

Q: Do Communist cadres know about your Christian meetings?

A: Sometimes they do. In some instances it is quite marvellous. For example, in our neighboring village the mother of the secretary of the production battalion is a Christian, so there was nothing that he could do. . . .

This report reveals at least three ways by which the Spirit of God is working in China in bringing His people under the name of Jesus: (1) Healing the sick by His power, (2) expelling demons by His Spirit, and (3) using the Chinese family system for evangelism. . . .

Chao's emphasis is on bringing Chinese people into the visible church, bringing them "under the name of Jesus."

A similar concern for the visible church is expressed by Father Domenico Grasso, S.J., in a book edited by Michael Chu, *New China: A Catholic Response.* Father Grasso opposes two statements which suggested that God's primary action might possibly be outside traditional church and mission structures. One was Hosea Williams' question, "Is it possible that God has become so disgusted with the 'believers' that he has decided to turn the moral future of mankind over to nonbelievers?" The other was an ex-China missionary's comment that "our mandate has been withdrawn," and "the end of the missionary era was the will of God." Writes Father Grasso:

We cannot, however, accept these opinions because they are contrary to the Bible which is the word of God for us. The word of truth entrusted to the Church must, with Christ's help, resound to the ends of the earth (Acts 1:8) and until the end of the world (Matt. 28:16-20). No. Humanity's religious future remains entrusted to the Church no matter how imperfect its members may be. God did not turn to nonbelievers; he has not taken back the mandate conferred on the apostles and their successors, the college of Bishops united to the Pope. The missionary era is not over and will not be over so long as there are people to be evangelized including those living in the New China.

In this vein, Protestant theologian Charles West writes:

> Evangelism must be a dimension of our Christian responsibility for China. Despite all our personal and social sins . . . we are called to make known the ways of the judge and redeemer of the world to all peoples. If there is not an evangelistic quality in our entire relation to other people and cultures we are not really being serious about the God in whom we claim to believe. Unless we care about, pray for, and support however we can the church in China in its mission, we are not really trying to respond to God's purposes there.

A common factor which holds these views together is the phrase *extra ecclesium nulla salus* or "outside the church no salvation." True, some in this camp may hold that a preliminary or partial or limited salvation may be possible in non-Christian contexts, but the visible church is necessary for the fullness of salvation, and this requirement is the most important factor to consider when viewing any situation, including China.

THE "LORD OF HISTORY" APPROACH

The second type of response falls loosely under the label "Lord of History," emphasizing God's action beyond the church. Most of those who take this path see the possibility of significant saving works of God being manifested in non-Christian, even anti-religious contexts. This group ranges from the pragmatic to the radical, that is, from those who simply observe things in China which seem to be of God and therefore to be affirmed to those who make this perception of God's action outside the church the grounds for quite new thinking.

A former Canadian missionary to China, E. H. Johnson, who made return visits in the 1970's, reflected on the accomplishments of the new government, then on Christian response:

> For Christians, what is happening to the people of China—a fourth of the human family—is profoundly important. We believe God created all, and is concerned to save all.
>
> I can't imagine, though, anything more counter-productive and showing less faith in the Holy Spirit than blasting in the Gospel from the Philippines or Bible smuggling, as some suggest. These are part of the devious ways in which the West established its domination in the past. . . .
>
> I suggest these guidelines:
>
> 1. Don't mount a missionary team ready to flood into China when the doors are open. The doors may never again be open to certain kinds of foreign missions.
>
> 2. Wait until the Church in China reaches out a hand for help. Its big-

gest problem is not the government but the question of how Christians express themselves in relation to the new society.

3. Listen to the lessons China has for the church. Try to understand its radical transformation of political, ideological, social and religious structures.

4. Prepare men and women now in Chinese language and knowledge of contemporary China to be ready for whatever the future calls for.

Another former missionary, Earl Willmott, goes further in suggesting the possibility of faith even for an atheist. Willmott writes:

The heroic old peasant who led his production brigade to turn their rockstrewn valley into terraced fields told of his own emancipation and said, "But if a person thinks only of his own emancipation and happiness, he may perhaps slide down the wrong road." I realized I had not heard a Chinese speak of seeking happiness. Perhaps a life of devoted serving has no need to seek personal goals.

Is not all this like Jesus' teaching? In their dedication to act "for the good of the people," are the Chinese people not committed to "doing the will of God"—though with no knowledge of the name of "God"? Consider Jesus' parable of the two sons. When the father asked them to go and work in the fields, the first said "no" but he went; the second said, "I go," but did not. Jesus asked, "Which did the will of his father?" In 1950 in Chengtu I heard two Chinese pastors preach on this parable; both suggested that Christians were so often like the second son, while the leaders of the revolution, who say "no" to God, were like the first.

And that raises a question. Is it not possible to have faith in God and yet not believe in the idea of God? We might reflect on this quotation from the French Marxist, Roger Garaudy: "What gives meaning, beauty and value to life, is for the Marxist as for the Christian, to give oneself without any limit to what the world, through our sacrifice, can become." Somehow I cannot help thinking they have been more successful in China than in the Christian church in the West in bringing people into this life-giving experience.

In the examples given above the authors, former China missionaries, have seen something positive in China and are grappling with the question of how to respond. Theologian C.S. Song takes up this whole issue of "salvation outside the church." The unwillingness of Western Christians to see "saving value" in non-Christian cultures is felt to be a subtle way of maintaining a Western imperialist stand. China causes trauma because it challenges the very notion of Western superiority and in doing so forces us to look at our Christian roots in a new way. "What does it mean," asks

C.S. Song, "when atheistic Communist regimes . . . act as liberators from poverty, starvation, social injustices, and human indignity?" It means that we have to see the life of the church differently. "An understanding of Christian mission in terms of evangelizing and converting the pagans and bringing them into the fold of the church is irrelevant in the context of modern China," concludes Song. The prophet Isaiah saw Cyrus, a Persian, as an agent of salvation. "Unless we, like Isaiah . . . begin to see those alien to our faith as making a contribution to the development of human community, as agents of God, our reading of history will be one-sided. . . ." Many would see Mao Tse-tung in a role analogous to that of Cyrus.

Francis Sullivan, Jesuit writer, comments on the view of C.S. Song and others whom, he says, give a secular definition of salvation—seeing it as "liberation," "humanization," or "freedom to be human." Sullivan feels that this approach, which refuses to center salvation in the institutional church, may be truer to a Christian understanding of God. By rejecting a church-centered idea of salvation they opt for what is really a more God-centered one, writes Sullivan. God is given a more central role in salvation history because God's acts of salvation are found not only in "sacred" contexts but in every process of genuine liberation and humanization, even in China, where God's very existence is denied. Sullivan says that this concept of salvation is sound as long as salvation is seen as an ongoing process and not a final accomplished fact in some social movement. God's saving action, he says, can be recognized "in every event of human history whereby people are saved and freed from any of the various forms of bondage and oppression to which 'the sin of the world' has subjected them."

Father Sullivan sees salvation as broader and more inclusive than just salvation of the soul. The liberation of humanity from sinful structures of oppression and exploitation is truly a work of salvation. "As Israel came gradually to understand that Yahweh was not just a tribal god, but the God of all nations and people, so also we have to understand that Christ . . . is Lord not just over the 'Christian' nations, but over all peoples, whether they know him as Lord or not."

Another Catholic writer, Joachim Pillai, is also in the "Lord of History" group. Pillai writes:

> It is true that the central aspect of freedom, as freedom for God, . . . is absent in Mao's vision of liberation. But even here I would say that this dimension is not explicitly denied. . . . Just as God is not unambiguously present in the Christian political and ecclesiastical systems, so too He is not totally absent in the Communist phenomenon, if we know how to read between the lines and discern the presence of God at points of tension and liberation in society. Christ is really present there where men, women, and children are struggling to be human.

The "Lord of History" approach, we can see from these several authors, tries to move away from a narrow view of God which confines divine power to the visible church or equates it with Western culture. It sees the power of God at work in the world in many diverse ways and does not limit salvation to the Christian community.

THE CHRISTIAN AFFIRMATION OF MAOIST VALUES

The third response focuses on the "Christian" quality of Mao's values. It does not give a direct answer to the question of the visible church, although authors in this group may deal with that question in other contexts.

The essence of this response is the affirmation that the experience of the people in China today, their way of living and interacting, is in some way "Christian," aside from any considerations about religious adherence or belief.

Perhaps the most forthright expression of the Christian quality of Maoist values is in the writings of British Christian and scientist Joseph Needham:

> China is, I think, further on the way to the true society of mankind, the Kingdom of God if you like, than our own. . . . We don't know what back-slidings and failures will occur, but on the whole, I think they are more advanced.

> You will naturally ask about the situation of the Christian churches. They are exceedingly weak. . . . I don't believe there has been any great number of Christian martyrs. I am much more inclined to think that many Christians have felt that their aims were being implemented by revolutionary Chinese communism and that they ought to join up with it. . . .

> And so one comes to the great paradox that, as I see it, in China they are implementing the second great commandment far better than has been done by Christendom at any period, while at the same time rejecting altogether the first one. . . . I think China is the only truly Christian country in the world in the present day, in spite of its absolute rejection of all religion.

Carman St. J. Hunter has also pondered the Christian significance of Chinese values and writes of her encounter with China:

> Not only are values—such as friendship; co-operation; self-sacrifice; rigid honesty; full participation of women; moral persuasion as the means of social control; the breaking down of differences in the treatment and status of citizens; productive labour; trust in the intuition of the masses to embrace the good when the issues are understood—all proclaimed verbally, but they are also internalized as part of a total system of education. . . .

If values are criteria for interpersonal and communal life, beneath them lie the social and religious myths which provide their substance. Every society develops a way, or ways, of understanding and responding to deep existential forces—the mystery and deepest meaning at the centre of being; the inevitable experience of anguish and ecstasy; the tragic dimension in life. Myths develop from the history and experience of a people. They are an expression of how participant peoples see truth, but they are not truth itself. . . .

In China the Long March is not only an actual historical event, it is also basic to the dominant myth of the present society. It stands for the transforming journey from the old society to the new. It represents the long struggle against all the afflictions of humanity and holds the promise of final victory not only for the Chinese but for all the hopeless of the earth.

Those whose lives reflect the spirit of self-sacrifice and service to the people are revered by the masses and their story told over and over. Salvation is won through suffering. Death is given meaning within the movement of the whole people toward the new future. The Cultural Revolution, with its recognition of the growing dangers of elitism, is symbolic of a process that Christians might describe as recognition of sin, repentance, confession, forgiveness and expiation through reconversion to the ideals of revolution.

The "Christian" value-system of Maoist China is also perceptible in the comments of Wu Yi-fang, about changes since the revolution. The following is taken from a report written by Eugene Stockwell of the National Council of Churches.

Later in the morning four of us had a chance to talk with 83-year-old Wu Yi-fang, a distinguished and articulate woman who years ago, before 1949, was President of Ginling Women's College, a Christian university in Nanking. Over the years she gradually became impressed with the way the new government really helped people, beyond mere social service. She slowly became convinced of the rightness of Mao's thought, helped with provincial educational policies, and eventually became an enthusiastic supporter of the government. In time she gave up her Christian faith as well. Here we were talking to a very Christ-like woman, a beautiful person, who avowedly had given up her Christian faith. Two quotations stick with me. She is deeply impressed with the way neighbors help each other in the new society neighborhoods. The Chinese phrase is: "If there is difficulty in one place, then help comes from eight sides." The other comment related to Chairman Mao and Premier Chou En-lai, both of whom Mme. Wu admires greatly. She has concluded, admiring these men as well as the present new Chairman Hua, that "the basic qualification of a person is unselfishness." That is not too bad a Christian statement, for an ex-Christian non-Christian! One cannot help but recall the phrase, "By their fruits you shall know them."

William Small, a Canadian missionary in China from 1941 to 1952 who returned for a visit in 1973, reported on how he continued to find in China a learning experience for himself as a Christian.

> While those concerned with Christian values cannot take exception to the high moral principles espoused (in China) and, indeed, must be supportive of the objective promoted, the question of the means of bringing about desired change is clearly important and of concern. Though there was insistence on adherence to ultimate goals and at times excesses must have prevailed in dealing with subversive groups, persuasion was known to be the major instrument used in promoting the concept of the desired new man and the new society.
>
> China's many problems are far from resolution, but the pervasive atmosphere of self-confidence and enthusiasm, of discipline and dedication, of overriding collective purpose and cooperation, of constructive criticism and self-criticism suggest that this nation is on an historic mission. The short period last summer (1973) provided another significant learning experience and left me wondering how an avowedly atheistic regime could strongly emphasize so many humane qualities supporting the dignity and equality of man, and how our own society, with a large percentage of the population professing Christians and with the wide-spread influence of Christian institutions, was lacking in so many of the above-noted characteristics.

Raymond Fung, a Chinese Christian in Hong Kong, wrote after visiting China:

> There is a lot of interest in learning English. A taxi driver checked with me his pronunciation of "zoo" and "memorial" in order to "better serve the people." A cadre showed me the English translation of "Quotations from Chairman Mao," asking me point-blank whether the translation was in any way as good as the original. . . . I went over a quotation and suggested that the phrase "we must endeavor" could be replaced by "we must strive. . . ." The Communist seemed pleased. He took down the word and pronounced slowly in English, "We must strive to serve the people."
>
> Eventually, the trip was over. Near Sheung Shui in the British sector, beside the railway line, I saw a cross on a church wall. And then I suddenly came to realize that the cross can never make sense to my seven hundred million fellow Chinese unless we who claim to be Christians also can say honestly, "We must strive to serve the people." Or, cross or no cross, there is no audience.

Those who find worthy Christian values in China are often led to a searching attitude about how Christian faith influences society in the West. In 1976 a group of coal miners from Nova Scotia, a miner's chorus called "Men of the Deeps," toured China. They had the chance to see the life of

their counterparts, Chinese coal miners. They affirmed that "Chinese culture and values today resemble nothing so much as a religious society without God." One of the miners, an active Catholic layman, felt that "China
was, in effect, practicing Christian principles with a seriousness that few
Christians can match." In a late night conversation on a homeward bound
bus after the China trip he said to a friend:

> You know what bothers me? We're supposed to be a Christian society,
> and they're supposed to be an atheist society. But what kept coming to
> me again and again, and I couldn't get away from it, was this: I kept on
> feeling that, more than ours, their society was pleasing to God.

Many people then, coming from a variety of backgrounds, have felt that
values in China seem more "Christian" than those in the West. What one
does with such an observation is another problem. A British Christian
leader, Simon Barrington Ward, feels that values are not the whole
question:

> Too much talk about Mao's Christian values misses the point. Christian
> faith is not ultimately about values, which are still part of the Law. It is
> about grace. It is about the fact that healing of our contradictions and
> the reconciling of our oppositions must continually well up among us
> out of a love from beyond ourselves, out of . . . cross and resurrection.
> We are all indebted to the great stimulus of Mao's China. But perhaps
> it is in the as yet tiny but growing traces of a new, free, and practical
> Christianity (in China) . . . that we must discern the final clue of the
> meaning of the quest for true human fulfillment.

What Ward is doing here takes us back to the first group—the "visible
church" approach, since he finds the "final clue" to human fulfillment in
the small Christian communities in China. Others who are impressed by
Christian values in China might move toward the "Lord of History"
approach, giving less emphasis to the institutional church. Danish theologian Johannes Aagaard's view, for example, is quite different from
Ward's:

> Salvation today—in China? No need of the question mark. The King-
> dom of God—in China? How can it be questioned? But the church and
> missions in China? That is quite another matter, not unimportant, but
> not *that* important. A Norwegian old missionary lady once said, "Mao
> has done much good for China, and China is more important for God
> than the church in China." This is a true insight. God saves the world,
> and the church is meant to be an instrument of that salvation. But if it
> has become a bad instrument, it will be cast away. As an instrument it
> has no value in itself. And God can find new instruments of His salva-
> tion. That is not only so in China.

CHINA AS A MIRROR FOR REFLECTING ON CHRISTIAN LIFE AND MISSION

Another response to China is that which takes the Chinese experience as an occasion for thinking anew about theology and Christian life. Of course writers referred to in this category may also reflect on values, God in history, and the visible Church. What is of interest here is those persons, or those passages, which take such reflection as the central motif. China challenges many areas of our thinking about the mission of the church and the style of the Christian community life. This challenge may, in fact, be the most important aspect of our study of China.

Raymond Fung suggests that the experience of China may provide some new insights on mission thinking of importance to other parts of the world. The new approach, he suggests, would put primary emphasis on the missionary as a learner. The missionary would not be the expert who comes with "authority" but rather a learner who comes to be with those considered to be culturally equal. The People's Republic of China is culturally equal with the West. Foreigners, including Christians, should be prepared to learn and to relate as equals.

Eugene Stockwell after visiting China found that the experience raised many questions about community life of the church here in North America. He lists six questions which forced themselves upon him as he reflected as a Christian on what he witnessed in China:

1. What does the People's Republic of China teach us about the meaning of participatory democracy?

Though it is true that the Chinese government is authoritarian and directed from above, it is impressive to note the many ways in which the Chinese people, particularly at the local and community levels, determine their own destiny and participate in decision making about matters closest to them. Neighborhood committees, self criticism groups, study gatherings and all sorts of local organizations provide persons with what seem to be almost too many opportunities to think through their own activities and determine their day to day tasks. The concept of "democratic centralism" as applied to production goals for communes and factories means that production targets initiated by central economic planning are eventually received at local commune and factory levels for ample discussion, amendment, alternative suggestions and potential new directions. Thus, peasants and workers participate actively in many of the detailed plans that most immediately affect their work life. As we compare this reality with what occurs in the West I cannot help but wonder whether employees on large farms or in large industries in the West have really as much to say about their work and future as the Chinese do.

2. How does the People's Republic of China challenge our concepts of justice?

As we traveled in China, we from the United States tended to ask one wrong question: "What is your salary?" Often skilled Chinese professionals, such as surgeons or teachers, would respond with a blank look wondering why this question was asked. If the basic motivation for work is to "Serve The People" then the matter of monetary reward for the service is quite secondary. What in fact happens in China is that people are paid financially for their services within certain minimum and maximum ranges, none of which are high by U.S. standards, for the fundamental criteria is justice for all so that no one should starve and no one should be rich at the expense of others. The result is a fundamental justice which extends to pay scales but also to many other areas of life where it is expected that no person or family will have greater rewards than others. This is not to suggest that perfect justice has been achieved in China but it is to say that in principle and in intention Chinese society places the concept of justice at the heart of its system. One could wish that in Western societies some such commitment to justice might be as evident.

3. How does the People's Republic of China challenge our views of freedom?

One of the recurring questions as we traveled through China was: "What does freedom mean?" We could see that the Chinese are often assigned tasks that they may or may not want. Freedom to travel from one area of the country to the other or outside of the country is strictly controlled. It is said there is considerable freedom of thought but as one views "cultural performances" one sometimes wonders whether artistic freedom is real. On the other hand, indiscriminate license is barred so that people do not have the "freedom" to kill themselves with drugs or to starve or to be degraded by others. Freedom is seen not simply in individualistic terms but is seen in terms of the dignity of the whole community and nation. Freedom also means lack of subservience to foreign governments and the ability to stand as an equal in the world community.

4. In what ways does the People's Republic of China help us to understand the nature of what is "political"?

In the West we tend to separate politics out from much of the rest of our life whereas in China all of life is seen to be intentionally related to political decisions that affect the total community. If one is concerned for the whole community or for the improvement of that community it is unavoidable that political activity be at the heart of change or improvement. The Chinese social system suggests to Westerners that we be more realistic about our political options and responsibilities. It also suggests to Western observers who consider themselves to be Christian that there is no possibility of separating out a religious faith from the choices of political options because if faith is concerned with the whole person and the community it must deal with the political choices the person and community must make.

5. How does the People's Republic of China press us to understand the ways God works in history?

It is not easy to determine exactly how God works in the history of any nation. I believe that during the last quarter century God has not been absent or far from the Chinese people. I believe that the vast social improvements in China are the work of the Holy Spirit and even among those who call themselves atheists and would not acknowledge the Holy Spirit. Also, a part of God's work in China may be to challenge us in the West to relook at our own social system where injustice or repression is institutionalized or condoned.

6. As we look at the People's Republic of China, are we not pressed to ask new and profound questions about ourselves and our society? If so, how do we begin to ask appropriate questions about ourselves and our society?

We do not have to use the Chinese society as a model for the West and, indeed, the Chinese warned against a description of their society as a "model." However, there are large questions raised for us as we compare our social institutions and systems with those of the Chinese. One question, for instance: Are our nations and societies of the West deeply committed to justice and fairness for all, the abolition of drugs and other factors which destroy human life, the abolition of hunger and the search for human dignity for every person. Because nearly a quarter of the human race has been able to institutionalize some of these commitments in daily life and community organization, it would seem that the rest of the human race could move toward similar commitments even though all the ideo-

logical baggage and political system of the PRC are not swallowed whole. May it not be that in the West we could begin to address the fundamental human and humane questions the Chinese society has been wrestling with in recent years so that priority in our efforts might be given to the improvement of the lot of people on a just basis rather than to such matters as nuclear defense, the arms race, and protection of opportunities for the privileged to maintain their privileges and so on?

These question also require us to look at Chinese history again in the light of the biblical message. The re-telling of the story of the Good Samaritan, by Jonas Jonson, gives a new perspective on the Chinese experience:

A country, a culture, was on its way through the centuries. It fell in with robbers, who stripped it, beat it, and left it at the roadside half dead. The robbers were many: graft and corruption, war lords and generalissimos, foreign powers, Western merchants and missionaries. And China was helpless. A priest passed by: a Christian or a Buddhist or a representative of any other established religion, too concerned with religion to be willing to get his hands dirty with social reform and politics, not to speak of the violence required to put China on its feet.

A Levite, another religious professional, also passed by on the other side. Was he one of those well-meaning and informed people who see the need but have no means of changing the situation? Was he proceeding to Jericho to ask others to come and help, like all those pleading with Western countries to assist China? Was he a Confucian, more concerned with the preservation of the moral and social position of the elite than with the plight of the downtrodden, the poor and the exploited?

Finally the Samaritan arrived on the scene, one who was despised by the political and religious authorities, an outcast with no respectability. In Chinese eyes, he could be no other than Mao Tse-tung and the Chinese Communist Party. The wounds made by the imperialist robbers were healed, national dignity was restored, and armed protection was given. Here was the neighbour, the comrade, who was willing to go down into the ditch and lift the robbed and wounded from below. Here was the one deserving the love of the people and setting the example for a life style and a political programme.

Perhaps from the Wisdom Literature of the Hebrew scriptures we can discover some wisdom on China and Christian consciousness. Mission theologian Katharine Hockin, who was born in China and served there as a missionary, thinks so. The following section is her reflection on Ecclesiastes, China, and the Christian community.

Koheleth, the Preacher, writes in Ecclesiastes that God has made every-thing "beautiful" in its own time. He reflects on the appropriateness of different human activities in varied situations:
"For everything there is a season, and a time for every matter under heaven;
— a time to be born and a time to die;
— a time to plant, and a time to pluck up what is planted;
— a time to kill and a time to heal;
— a time to break down and a time to build up. . . ."

(Eccles. 3:1ff)

Popular folk thought and song make these words familiar. It is interest-ing that this Wisdom writer, who lived about three centuries before the Christian era, was doing for his day the reflection on life which is so modish in our own day as the "Action/Reflection Life-style." The biblical wisdom, frozen by posterity into tight, compact, almost quaint proverbs, when seen in this more dynamic context does bring us insights which are missed when these writings are seen simply as collected precepts.

All this relates specifically to North American Christian understanding of China today. The great years of Western missionary expansion assumed that the "Christian nations" had the responsibility to carry the gospel throughout the world. There was a particular urgency since without this agency there would be vast geographical areas where Christ would never be known. The agents of mission were generally people of white skin and of some variety of European heritage—from the "Christian civilizations."

By mid-twentieth century, when the People's Republic of China started on her new course under the administration of the Chinese Communist Party, the missionary enterprise had been forced to discover themes such as "Mission in Six Continents" and "Partnership in Mission." We of the West are still struggling with the implications of this reality. Our "mana-gerial attitudes" make it difficult for us to relax enough to be, in truth, partners and sharing comrades in a witness which (in Ecclesiastes' sense) is *timely*, having the deep appropriateness summoned by God's beautiful creation!

And how does China relate to these themes? When the Korean War hastened the withdrawal of Western personnel from China, we spoke of this door "closing" to Christian witness. A book written at the time was "The Lost Churches of China." They were lost to us, the old friends We thought they were lost to God as well. After all, were we not His servants and messengers?

In 1951 the North American churches researched the "Lessons from China." On the whole, the learnings of that study were personal and individual, not structural. Missionaries failed as people to recognize the values of other cultures. There was the failure, too, to shed paternalistic attitudes and privileged standards of living. The entanglement of mission policy with the expansion of colonialism was recognized and regretted. The analysis went only part way, though, in recognizing how this affected the credibility of the Western missionary enterprise.

The *Chinese Christian,* as one analyst of that time pointed out, was often attracted to the egalitarian policies of the new government *because* of his or her Christian conscience. This led to a division between foreign missionary and national colleague. We struggled to understand how significant segments of the Christian community under Communist rule could affirm their civil loyalty. To North American Christians, Communist rule seemed to demand Christian protest. *We* saw a nation ruled by leaders who denied the reality of Deity. *Chinese Christians* saw the work of a government on behalf of the disadvantaged.

We were challenged to shift grounds in the quest for understanding. "How can we perceive the signs of the times, and what God is doing in China as the sovereign ruler of human history?" The ground of consideration became the whole China scene, rather than the narrower focus on our daughter church.

One Christian visitor to China was particularly interested in trying to meet Christians and to visit church buildings, with a one-track flow of questions and requests. Finally the tour guide, who had been trying to let the visitor know about the achievements of the Chinese people in many areas of their life, responded with a bit of exasperation, "Are you only interested in this tiny minority of believers in our country? Have you no concern for anything but a group in which you people have an old vested interest?" We assumed the world existed for the strengthening of the church. Now it is necessary to realize that the church exists for the World. We must reflect on the relationship of the Chinese experience to God's purposes for human life.

To look at the panorama and quality of a people's life in order to learn from it is different from seeing only the potentialities for conversion and saving of souls. As the canvas stretches more widely we gain a new awareness of salvation activity to which we were previously blind. From the noted scientist Joseph Needham to the Cape Breton coal miners came the recognition that ordinary Chinese society has achieved more neighborly concern and interpersonal justice than most other nations of the world today. Such impressions and opinions may not be accepted easily. They have to be taken seriously, however, if one is concerned with faithfulness in mission. For we, who are committed to the effort to achieve a world which is really "beautiful" in God's eyes, must be challenged by any situation which can be appraised so positively.

It becomes clear that God and the ever-creative roving Spirit can find expression through a nation with which Western Christians have lost connection. Surprisingly perhaps, God's mission does go forward and without us as leading participants. (Can you not hear a compassionate and amused chuckle from somewhere in the heavenly places, as a divine parent sees some beloved but blinkered children begin to grow up *in* the family of humanity?) Does this not help us to discover new dimensions of that Mission, particularly where managerial attitudes are quite clearly impossible? Surely this points to a greater mutuality as we Western Christians discover appropriate and timely roles in the interrelated globe of the late seventies and eighties.

The message of wholeness which the gospel brings to the world is now carried in part by the achievements of a land which has picked up the practical service ideals expressed through Christian schools, hospitals and institutions. These have been woven into the fabric of the expressed goals of a whole society "in the service of the people." These goals, far from achieved, remain the base of practice to such a measure that the "China model" is taken seriously by many Third World nations today, which is, in turn, a challenge to us.

The message to us from many quarters today is, "You are part of our problem, not of its solution!" In the developmental debates regarding food, trade, aid or exchange, this conclusion is repeatedly affirmed. A creative and timely activity for the corporate structures of mission in the West today might be a profound and honest analysis of our history in mission. There was offered a great measure of obedience to God and there were achievements and productivity to the praise of God's name. We have also made mistakes and fumbled badly. When these errors are examined, accepted and forgiven, we might be enabled to participate in the mission of the future much more effectively.

It is easy to be burdened with guilt. This leads to hopelessness and anger. But guilt transcended by a confessional stance before God, and by seeking peace with our fellows, is liberating. It leads to greater freedom and obedience and also to a new quality of relationship with those from whom we are now alienated and estranged. If the Chinese experience could take us, under God, in this direction, we might indeed discover that there

is a time and season for all things under heaven, and that God's appropriate
time makes all things beautiful.

SOME QUESTIONS ON CHINA FOR CHRISTIANS IN SEARCH OF COMMUNITY

Readers may want to consider the following questions as they study life
in China.

Are there signs of God's saving grace in Maoist China? We have looked
at various aspects of life in China that have impressed people like the
Lings, who lived there nine years, as well as visitors on brief tours. Insofar
as wholesome community life is being fostered in China it seems to be
consistent with a Christian understanding of our life together. If this sense
of community in China is not of God, then what is its source? If it is,
what does that lead us to in our thinking about God's action in the world?

Should Christians sacrifice self for the sake of community? The Chinese
model, that of self-giving in order to serve the people, may not be lived
fully by many people in China, but it is the ideal. How do we respond to
that ideal as Christians? Do we agree with it or reject it? Why? Are our
cultural values ("Take care of Number One") consistent with our Christian values? Which are closer to values in China?

How do we respond to Chinese Marxist atheism? Does the atheism of
China need to be more of a barrier than differences we have with other
non-Christians? As Christians, are we closer to the atheist who acts justly
or to one who believes in God while treating people miserably?

Should Christians from the West seek to evangelize China? There might
be a "time to keep silence," as is suggested in Ecclesiastes; silence in which
to reflect on the past and on the future. Is it possible that our own mistakes of the past have created a time in which honest evangelism is
impossible? Probably anything we say now about Christianity will be mis-
understood in China. Would mounting some kind of Christian onslaught,
a new mission campaign for China, simply delay the time when any mean-
ingful communication can take place?

Where is there fullness of salvation? If we look at our own community
life, or that of China, we can see that fullness of salvation cannot be
claimed by any society. We are involved in continuing search and struggle.
But if completeness is absent in both China and our own society, might
it not be useful to have a dialogue about what each of us is discovering in
our search? Maybe China is not ready for such dialogue with Christians—
but are we Christians ready for dialogue with Chinese Marxists?

Where should Christians search for a new understanding of community? China does not have the answers for our questions. Rather, China's experience raises questions which lead us back to the biblical roots of our own faith. If we are able to see how God acts beyond the church, if we are humble enough to see that we do not have a monopoly on goodness, if we can open our minds to a very different experience like that of China, if we can hear the biblical message which comes to us as members of communities as well as individuals, then perhaps we are on our way to finding the community for which we search.

REPLY TO COMRADE KUO MO-JO

January 9, 1963

On this tiny globe
A few flies dash themselves against the wall,
Humming without cease,
Sometimes shrilling,
Sometimes moaning.
Ants on the locust tree assume a great-nation swagger
And mayflies lightly plot to topple the giant tree.
The west wind scatters leaves over Changan,
And the arrows are flying, twanging.

So many deeds cry out to be done,
And always urgently;
The world rolls on,
Time presses.
Ten thousand years are too long,
Seize the day, seize the hour!

The Four Seas are rising, clouds and waters raging,
The Five Continents are rocking, wind and thunder
        roaring.
Our force is irresistible,
Away with all pests!

Mao Tse-tung